LSU

DAILY DEVOTIONS FOR DIE-HARD FANS

TIGERS

Daily Devotions for Die-Hard Fans: LSU Tigers
© 2010 Ed McMinn

Library of Congress Cataloging-in-Publication Data
13 ISBN Digit ISBN: 978-0-9840847-2-2

Manufactured in the United States of America.

For bulk purchases or to request the author for speaking engagements,
email contact@extrapointpublishers.com.

Go to http://www.die-hardfans.com for information about other titles in
the series.

Cover and interior design by Slynn McMinn.

TIGERS

*Dedicated
to the
Greater Glory
of God*

IN THE BEGINNING

Read Genesis 1, 2:1-3.

"God saw all that he had made, and it was very good" (v. 1:31).

Blame it all on the ancient Greeks and a young chemistry professor who idealized their concept of the "whole" man. "It all," of course, is LSU football.

Charles E. Coates learned his football and his chemistry at Johns Hopkins University, which fielded its first team in 1882. When he arrived at the Louisiana Seminary of Learning and Military Academy to teach, he was surprised by the lack of athletics he found. Coates felt the purpose of a college education was to produce a "whole" man in the Greek fashion. That whole man included both scholarship and athletics.

So in the fall of 1893, he and Dr. H.A. Morgan, who was later president of the University of Tennessee, set out to change the situation. They enlisted some players, and in mid-November, LSU's first-ever football team began preparing for its first-ever game. The players had no uniforms; they nailed cleats on leather shoes.

The daily scrimmages began to generate some excitement around town, especially when the first game was scheduled: a contest on Nov. 25, 1893, against Tulane at Sportsman's Park in New Orleans. The *Baton Rouge Daily Advocate* published the state's first-ever football special edition, informing fans of special

TIGERS

round-trip train rates of $1.50 to New Orleans and of ticket prices for the game of 50 cents each. "Of course," the paper declared, "all Baton Rougeans will cheer lustily for the cadets."

The afternoon was cold and cloudy; the crowd was estimated at between 1,500 and 2,000. Each team named one official for the game with the Louisiana team selecting Professor Coates. Tulane had already played a game and it showed. They won 34-0.

After that first game, LSU hired a paid coach, Albert P. Simmons, and whipped Tulane 8-4 in 1895, the next time they played.

Beginnings are important, but what we make of them is even more important. Consider, for example, how far the LSU football program has come since that first season. Every morning, you get a gift from God: a new beginning. God hands to you as an expression of divine love a new day full of promise and the chance to right the wrongs in your life. You can use the day to pay a debt, start a new relationship, replace a burned-out light bulb, tell your family you love them, chase a dream, solve a nagging problem . . . or not.

God simply provides the gift. How you use it is up to you. People often talk wistfully about starting over or making a new beginning. God gives you the chance with the dawning of every new day. You have the chance today to make things right – and that includes your relationship with God.

It struck me we ought to have that sort of thing.
-- Dr. Charles E. Coates, speaking of football at LSU

Every day is not just a dawn; it is a precious chance to start over or begin anew.

SMART MOVE

Read 1 Kings 4:29-34; 11:1-6.

"[Solomon] was wiser than any other man. . . . As Solomon grew old, his wives turned his heart after other gods, and his heart was not fully devoted to the Lord his God" (vv. 4:31, 11:4).

National championship game. So the coach decides to bat in the crucial four spot a part-time player who hadn't been hitting much even when he played. What kind of move is that? Turned out to be a smart one.

After starting 41 of the first 42 games of the 2009 baseball season, junior first baseman Sean Ochinko's run production was down so much that Coach Paul Mainieri left him off the 25-man roster when the Tigers played Auburn in late April. Since then he had been platooned, batting sixth or seventh, and had driven in only four runs in the season's final sixteen games.

Then in the decisive third game of the College World Series championship against Texas, Mainieri made what at first glance sure didn't seem like a smart move. He not only put Ochinko in the lineup, but he had him bat fourth, a spot Ochinko had not occupied since April 22.

The move worked out quite well. Ochinko went 4-for-5 with three singles, a mammoth ninth-inning home run that wrapped up the 11-4 win for the national championship, and three RBIs.

Mainieri said he had a method to his madness that was key

TIGERS

to the Tigers' sixth national title. He moved Ochinko into the cleanup slot to protect the designated hitter, Blake Dean, whom opponents had pretty much pitched around in the College World Series. Ochinko didn't waste any time demonstrating just how smart Mainieri's move was. He drilled the first pitch he saw for a base hit. Jared Mitchell followed up with a three-run homer.

We don't always make smart moves, do we? Remember that time you wrecked the car when you spilled hot coffee on your lap? That cold morning you fell out of the boat? The time you gave your honey a tool box for her birthday?

Formal education notwithstanding, we all make some dumb moves sometime because time spent in a classroom is not an accurate gauge of common sense. Folks impressed with their own smarts often grace us with erudite pronouncements that we intuitively recognize as flawed, unworkable, or simply wrong.

A good example is the observation that great intelligence and scholarship are not compatible with faith in God. That is, the more we know, the less we believe. But any incompatibility occurs only because we begin to trust in our own wisdom rather than the wisdom of God. We forget, as Solomon did, that God is the ultimate source of all our knowledge and wisdom and that even our ability to learn is a gift from God.

Not smart at all.

He told me he wasn't going to let me down, and he didn't.
-- Coach Paul Mainieri on Sean Ochinko's batting fourth

Being truly smart means trusting in God's wisdom rather than only in our own knowledge.

BLUEGRASS MIRACLE

Read Matthew 12:38-42.

"He answered, 'A wicked and adulterous generation asks for a miraculous sign!'" (v. 39)

Kentucky students were flooding the field to celebrate a win; the Wildcat head coach had already been soaked with Gatorade; the network televising the game had already flashed the final score on the screen: Kentucky 30 LSU 27. Only it was all wrong. None of it took the Bluegrass Miracle into account.

On Nov. 9, 2002, at Commonwealth Stadium, LSU trailed Kentucky 30-27 with only two seconds left to play. The Tigers were at their own 25, and the Kentucky fans and players had begun a full-fledged victory celebration.

But then Devery Henderson entered Tiger folklore with a "Hail Mary" miracle on a play that the team had practiced repeatedly for months -- without success.

Quarterback Marcus Randall let the pigskin fly with all the arm strength he had. It sailed 68 yards and came down "in a blur of blue, white, and gold colors." A Wildcat safety got a finger on it, a linebacker also touched it, and a cornerback tipped it. The fourth -- and final -- player to touch the ball was Henderson.

He snatched it out of the air at the 18, juggled the ball for several steps, and then ran through an attempted tackle and into the end zone as time ran out.

"We practice that play every week," Henderson said. "But it

never works." It didn't really work against Kentucky either. As "Dash-right-93 Berlin" was designed, Henderson was to tip the ball to receiver Michael Clayton. Instead, everyone was out of position, and the tip guy turned out to be a Kentucky player.

"It was like a dream," Henderson said. "I couldn't believe it." Neither could the Wildcats and their fans, their party crashed suddenly by the Bluegrass Miracle.

Miracles -- like a game-winning touchdown on the last play -- defy rational explanation. Escaping with minor abrasions from an accident that totals your car merits being termed "miraculous." So is recovering from an illness that seemed terminal. Underlying the notion of miracles is that they are rare instances of direct divine intervention that reveal God.

But life shows us quite the contrary, that miracles are anything but rare. Since God made the world and everything in it, everything around you is miraculous. Even you are a miracle. Your life can be mundane, dull, and ordinary, or it can be spent in a glorious attitude of childlike wonder and awe. It depends on whether or not you see the world through the eyes of faith. Only through faith can you discern the hand of God in any event; only through faith can you see the miraculous and thus see God.

Jesus knew that miracles don't produce faith, but rather faith produces miracles.

It was just a freak, unbelievable thing.
  -- LSU offensive coordinator Jimbo Fisher on the Bluegrass Miracle

**Miracles are all around us,
but it takes the eyes of faith to see them.**

HEART AND SOUL

Read Romans 12:1-2.

"Therefore, I urge you, brothers, in view of God's mercy, to offer your bodies as living sacrifices, holy and pleasing to God – this is your spiritual act of worship" (v. 1).

When quarterback Matt Flynn committed to LSU before his senior season, he really committed.

Flynn arrived in Baton Rouge in 2003 to find JaMarcus Russell there too. For four years, including a redshirt season, Flynn basically sat on the bench, playing behind Russell the last three. He held for extra points and field goals and took some snaps "in garbage time." He was tempted to transfer, frustrated by his lack of playing time and the knowledge that his parents faithfully drove 333 miles from Tyler, Texas, to Baton Rouge for all the games only to see him play very little.

He had made a commitment, though. LSU was where he wanted to be, and so he "stubbornly" waited for his time.

That time arrived with the 2007 season when Russell left early for the pros. A senior, Flynn quarterbacked the Tigers to the SEC championship game, though he missed it with a shoulder injury suffered in the season finale against Arkansas.

He was ready, however, for the national championship game on Jan. 7. He threw four touchdown passes in the 38-24 romp over Ohio State, his perfect pass to wideout Brandon LaFell in the left corner of the end zone giving the Tigers their first lead after they

TIGERS

had fallen behind early 10-0.

At last, Matt Flynn could celebrate the rewards brought his way by his commitment. He was named the game's offensive MVP. "This isn't how I would have scripted my career coming out of high school," Flynn admitted. "It's been tough, but right now it's so, so sweet."

When you stood in a church and recited your wedding vows, did you make a decision that you could walk away from when things got tough or did you make a lifelong commitment? Is your job just a way to get a paycheck, or are you committed to it?

Commitment seems almost a dirty word in our society these days, a synonym for chains, an antonym for freedom. Perhaps this is why so many people are afraid of Jesus: Jesus demands commitment. To speak of offering yourself as "a living sacrifice" is not to speak blithely of making a decision but of heart-body-mind-and-soul commitment.

But commitment actually means "purpose and meaning," especially when you're talking about your life. Commitment makes life worthwhile. Anyway, in insisting upon commitment, Jesus isn't asking anything from you that he hasn't already given to you himself. His commitment to you was so deep that he died for you.

I wouldn't give up this one year for four years starting anywhere else.
-- Matt Flynn

**Rather than constraining you,
commitment to Jesus lends meaning to your life,
releasing you to move forward with purpose.**

DAY 5

A SURE THING

Read Romans 8:28-30.

"We know that in all things God works for the good of those who love him, who have been called according to his purpose" (v. 28).

Glenn Holt was a sure thing. Wendell Davis was not. Yet Davis wound up the All America (See Devotion No. 54.) and Holt left LSU. In one of life's strange twists, the reversal happened because the lines on Tiger Stadium were irregular.

Holt was "an up-and-coming LSU receiver" in the spring of 1985. Davis had not caught a single pass as a freshman. Clearly, Holt was LSU's next star. But life didn't turn out that way.

Until 1985, there was little running room outside the north end zone in Tiger Stadium. A player quickly ran into a fence. The south end zone, however, "had several yards of cushion between the end marker and fence." That irregular field marking was corrected in time for the 1985 season to allow for five more yards of running room in that short north end zone.

It was too late for Holt, however. During spring training in 1985, he made a reception in the north end zone and couldn't stop himself in time to keep from slamming into the fence. He put out his hand to halt his momentum. The blow broke that hand.

Davis, Holt's best friend, took over his starting job. When the injury healed, Holt could never reclaim the starting position. He took ill, eventually left LSU, and faded from memory while Davis

TIGERS

went on to a stellar career both in college and in the pros.

During the spring of 1987, the two accidentally met each other on a street corner in Orlando, Fla. "We were both shocked," Davis recalled. Holt was on the track team at Western Kentucky. Davis was on his way to a photo session for a preseason All-America team. They made small talk, Holt offered Davis congratulations for his success, and the two friends went their separate ways.

Neither one's life had turned out the way everyone expected.

Football games aren't played on paper. That is, you attend an LSU game expecting the Tigers to win, but you don't know for sure. If you did, why bother to go? Any football game worth watching carries with it an element of uncertainty.

Life doesn't get played on paper either, which means that living, too, comes laden with uncertainty. You never know what's going to happen tomorrow or even an hour from now. Oh, sure, you think you know. For instance, right now you may be certain that you'll be at work Monday morning or that you'll have a job next month. Life's uncertainties, though, can intervene at any time and disrupt your nice, pat expectations.

Ironically, while you can't know for sure about this afternoon, you can know for certain about forever. Eternity is a sure thing because it's in God's hands. Your unwavering faith and God's sure promises lock in a certain future for you.

There is nothing in life so uncertain as a sure thing.
-- NHL Coach Scotty Bowman

Life is unpredictable and tomorrow is uncertain;
only eternity is a sure thing
because God controls it.

THE MOTHER LODE

Read John 19:25-30.

"Near the cross of Jesus stood his mother" (v. 25).

Five times a day. That's how often Sylvia Fowles called her mother when she was at LSU.

Fowles was a key component of the most successful run in LSU women's basketball history and one of the greatest runs in NCAA Tournament lore. In 2008, the Lady Tigers joined Connecticut as the only team in NCAA women's basketball history to advance to five straight Final Fours. Fowles played on four of those teams.

She finished her career in Baton Rouge in 2008 as the SEC career leader in rebounds and the school career leader in blocked shots, free throws made, and games played. She was a two-time All-America and the SEC Player of the Year as a senior. She was the second player selected in the 2008 pro draft.

At 6'6", "Big Syl" was no shrinking violet. Coach Van Chancellor once described her journeys into the lane as "jungle excursions that require a machete 'to cut through all the grasping vines.'"

Still, the Fowles who played at LSU was at heart a gentle soul who determinedly sought to fulfill her mission of "bringing a bit of sunshine into the lives of everyone she encounter[ed]." When children too timid to ask her for an autograph approached her, she usually swept them into her long arms and hugged them. "She'll hug grown people too," teammate RaShonta LeBlanc said. "Even people she's never met before."

TIGERS

That gentleness included devotion to her mother and thus the five calls a day. The youngest of five children, Fowles was raised in one of the most dangerous neighborhoods in Miami. "My mom did everything she could to raise us like a normal family," Fowles said. "Inside the house we had everything we wanted. Outside was tough. You saw a lot of things kids aren't supposed to see."

So at LSU, Sylvia Fowles, the mama's girl, returned that love and devotion by staying in constant contact.

Mamas often do what Sylvia Fowles' mother did: overcome exceptional challenges to give their children a chance for a better life. No mother in history, though, has faced a challenge to match that of Mary, whom God chose to be the mother of Jesus. Like mamas and their children throughout time, Mary experienced both joy and perplexity in her relationship with her son.

To the end, though, Mary stood by her boy. She followed him all the way to his execution, an act of love and bravery since Jesus was condemned as an enemy of the Roman Empire.

But just as mothers like Mary and Sylvia Fowles' – and perhaps yours -- would apparently do anything for their children, so will God do anything out of love for his children. After all, that was God on the cross at the foot of which Mary stood, and he was dying for you, one of his children.

Everyone should find time to write and to go see their mother. I think that's healthy.

– Bear Bryant

**Mamas often sacrifice for their children,
but God, too, will do anything out of love
for his children, including dying on a cross.**

RAIN CHECK

Read Genesis 9:8-17.

*"I establish my covenant with you: Never again will all
life be cut off by the waters of a flood; never again will
there be a flood to destroy the earth" (v. 11).*

For all the glory with which it proceeded and eventually ended,
the 2003 LSU football season began rather ominously.

On Aug. 30, the 110th season of LSU football began with a home
game against UL-Monroe. The defense gave a quick indication of
how dominant it would be by quickly forcing the Warhawks to
punt. The Tigers didn't do much better, facing fourth and four on
their own 12 when suddenly the heavens above Tiger Stadium
put on a show. Lightning popped, thunder rolled, and the rain
came down in sheets. The combination forced a halt in play.

That was ominous enough as the Tiger faithful had to brave
the elements and wait out a 40-minute delay. Once play resumed,
though, the hearty fans still found little to cheer about as the Tiger
offense ominously sputtered through the first quarter.

After that, however, quarterback Matt Mauck "caught a bit of
the Louisiana lightning in a bottle," and the most remarkable
LSU season since 1958 was off and running toward the national
championship. "It was raining pretty hard at first and the field
was pretty slippery," Mauck said. "But I think as the game went
on, everybody on the whole team got more comfortable."

Especially Mauck. He threw an 8-yard touchdown pass to

TIGERS

wideout Devery Henderson, a 17-yard scoring toss to running back Joseph Addai, and a third TD strike to receiver Michael Clayton, all in the second quarter. He thus duplicated his own feat of being the only LSU quarterback in history to throw three touchdown passes in one quarter. LSU led 21-0 at halftime.

Despite the delay caused by the thunderstorm and the resulting wet field, the Tigers won easily 49-7.

The kids are on go for their picnic. Your golf game is set. You have rib eyes and smoked sausage ready for the grill when the gang comes over tonight. And then it rains.

Sometimes you can wait out a downpour and then slog on through the mud and the muck as LSU and UL-Monroe did. Often, however, the rain simply washes away your carefully laid plans, and you can't do anything about it.

Rain falls when and where it wants to without checking with you. It answers only to God, the one who controls the heavens from which it comes, the ground on which it falls, and everything in between -- territory that should include you. Though God has absolute dominance over the rain, he will take control of your life only if you let him. In daily seeking his will for your life, you discover that you can live so as to be walking in the sunshine even when it's raining.

Don't pray when it rains if you don't pray when the sun shines.
-- Pitcher and philosopher Leroy "Satchel" Paige

Into each life some rain must fall,
but you can live in the glorious light of God's love
even during a downpour.

THE FUNERAL

Read 1 Corinthians 15:50-57.

"'Death has been swallowed up in victory.' Where, O Death, is your victory? Where, O Death, is your sting?'" (vv. 54b-55)

They waited in a long line fifty deep to get inside, and when they did, they smiled and laughed -- just like Cholly Mac would have wanted it.

Charles McClendon was the head football coach at LSU from 1962-79, the longest tenure in school history. He won 137 games, the most of any Tiger coach. In 1970, he was the National Coach of the Year; he was inducted into the College Football Hall of Fame in 1986.

McClendon died of cancer in December 2001. Friends and former players packed the University Baptist Church for his funeral. What they remembered was a successful, upbeat, good-humored man whom they loved. "Coach Mac was really one of the great people in my life," declared LSU and NFL great Tommy Casanova. "Just to see the character and class that he had."

"Coach Mac gave everything he had," declared former Tiger quarterback Nelson Stokley who served as a McClendon assistant. "He was worried about others more than himself."

McClendon's voice was heard at his own funeral as he wrote part of his eulogy. "I would like to be remembered as a family man, father, grandfather who loved his family, friends, profession and life in general," he wrote. "I have prayed that what little I could contribute to our society would help make the place we live a little better."

Few present that December day would doubt that the world was "a little better" because Cholly Mac had been in it. "We lost a fine man," Paul Dietzel said, "but he'll never be forgotten."

Chances are you won't get the kind of send-off Charles McClendon did, one usually reserved for the likes of successful college football coaches and similar dignitaries. Still, you want a good funeral. You want a decent crowd, you want folks to shed some tears, and you want some reasonably distinguished-looking types to stand behind a lectern and say some very nice things about you. Especially if they're all true.

But have you ever been to a funeral where the deceased you knew and the deceased folks were talking about were two different people? Where everyone struggled to say something nice about the not-so-dearly departed? Or a funeral that was little more than an empty acknowledgement that death is the end of all hope. Sad, isn't it?

Exactly what does make a good funeral, one like Cholly Mac's where people laugh, love, and remember warmly and sincerely amid their tears? Jesus does. His presence transforms a mourning of death into a celebration of life.

I want my family, players and friends to only share tears of happiness today. Let's all remember the good times while we were together.
-- Charlie McClendon's message at his funeral

Amid tears there is hope; amid death
there is resurrection – if Jesus is at the funeral.

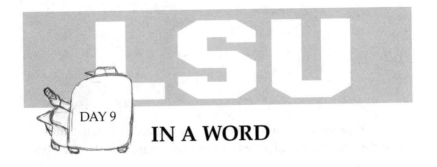

IN A WORD

Read Matthew 12:33-37.

"For out of the overflow of the heart the mouth speaks. The good man brings good things out of the good stored up in him, and the evil man brings evil things out of the evil stored up in him" (vv. 34b-35).

Words spoken in anger and in haste once cost LSU a football coach who didn't want to leave.

First as governor and then as senator, Huey Long was "a perennial sophomore when it came to LSU football." He would show up in the dressing room before games and pass out hamburgers. At halftime, he would lead the Tiger marching band down the field.

Thus, he ran out of patience after the Tigers lost 13-12 to Tulane -- which he particularly despised -- and Tennessee and trailed Oregon 13-0 at halftime in the final game of the 1934 season. He stormed into the dressing room and told Coach Biff Jones, "I'm sick of you losing games. You'd better win this one." Jones shot back, "Well, senator, get this: Win, lose or draw, I quit." "That's a bargain," Long retorted.

LSU came back to win 14-13, but Jones kept his word. He quit.

The only thing was that after the game was over, Jones didn't want to quit and Long didn't want him to. "They both said things they didn't mean," said Abe Mickal, then the Tiger quarterback (See devotion No. 65) and a lifelong friend of Jones'.

TIGERS

The Associated Press got wind of the halftime confrontation, which created a major problem. Mickal said, "Both Biff and Huey tried to get them to kill it, but AP wouldn't." Then once the story went public, "There was nothing anyone could do. Biff had to resign to save face; otherwise it would look like he was caving in. But he didn't want to leave."

Forced out by his own words, Jones left LSU with a fine 20-5-6 record in three seasons.

These days, everybody's got something to say and likely as not a place to say it. Talk radio, 24-hour sports and news TV channels, *Oprah, The View.* Talk has really become cheap.

But words still have power, and that includes not just those of the talking heads, hucksters, and pundits on television, but ours also. Our words are perhaps the most powerful force we possess for good or for bad. The words we speak today can belittle, wound, humiliate, and destroy. They can also inspire, heal, protect, and create. Our words both shape and define us. They also reveal to the world the depth of our faith.

We should never make the mistake of underestimating the power of the spoken word. After all, speaking the Word was the only means Jesus had to get his message across – and look what he managed to do.

We must always watch what we say, because others sure will.

You can motive players better with kind words than with a whip.
– Former College Football Coach Bud Wilkinson

Choose your words carefully; they are the most powerful force you have for good or for bad.

OUT WITH THE OLD

Read Hebrews 8:3-13.

"The ministry Jesus has received is as superior to theirs as the covenant of which he is mediator is superior to the old one, and it is founded on better promises" (v. 6).

LSU's softball players and coaches finally completed what was called "the longest one-mile move in program history."

That was in February 2009, when the new Tiger Park finally opened. Coach Yvette Girouard had begun lobbying for new softball facilities shortly after her hiring in 2001. Since 2004, she had been telling recruits they would be playing in a new state-of-the-art facility. Pitcher Emily Turner (2004-07), whose name is scattered all over the LSU record book, recalled that Girouard used the new stadium "as a way to recruit me. We were supposed to be the first class to play on the new field."

But several problems and setbacks -- including Hurricane Katrina -- delayed construction. All-American catcher Killian Roessner, who ended her career in 2008, never dreamed she would not play in the new stadium. Still, she wouldn't trade her time at LSU. "I'm glad I ended on the field I started on," she said.

But why was LSU so eager to throw away the old park and replace it with a new one? After all, "old" Tiger Park was only twelve years old, built just prior to the 1997 season, which marked the beginning of SEC/LSU softball. It wasn't like the team couldn't play in the park; the Tigers were an astounding 338-51 there.

TIGERS

But as Girouard explained, old Tiger Park was not a stadium, but a park. "We have no locker room here. For years, there were no bathrooms here. There was no place to park for fans." The old park cost $400,000 to build. "Every team in the SEC has a stadium that is worth well more than that."

As of Feb. 11, 2009, so did LSU. That's when the softball team christened the new Tiger Park with -- appropriately enough -- a win, 6-0 over McNeese St. The new had replaced the old.

Your car's running fine, but the miles are adding up. Time for a trade-in. Your TV set is still delivering a sharp picture, but those HDTV's are really something. Same with the newer computers. And how about those lawn mowers that turn on a dime?

Out with the old, in with the new — we're always looking for the newest thing on the market. In our faith life, that means the new covenant God gave us through Jesus Christ. An old covenant did exist, one based on the law God handed down to the Hebrew people. But God used this old covenant as the basis to go one better and establish a covenant available to the whole world. This new way is a covenant of grace between God and anyone who lives a life of faith in Jesus.

But don't get caught waiting for a newer, improved covenant; the promises God gave us through Jesus couldn't get any better.

Tiger Park by far is the most gorgeous stadium that I have ever seen. Our team is absolutely blessed to be playing here.
-- Tiger pitcher Kirsten Shortridge

**God's covenant through Jesus Christ
is plenty old, but don't look for
anything better to replace it.**

PRESSURE COOKER

Read 1 Kings 18:16-40.

"Answer me, O Lord, answer me, so these people will know that you, O Lord, are God" (v. 37).

Entering Louisiana. Set your watches back four seconds." So read a roadside sign erected by a disgruntled Rebel fan after one of the most exciting LSU-Ole Miss games in history.

The 1972 football season has been called the "Year of the Miracle" because of the Ole Miss game when Bert Jones "engineered the best pressure drive in Tiger Stadium history." The Rebels led 16-10 when LSU took over at its 20 with 3:01 and one time-out left.

Jones hit flanker Gerald Keigley with a 23-yard bullet to get the drive going. On fourth and two, Jones ignored the pressure to find Jimmy LeDoux for ten yards and a first down. He then hit sophomore tight end Brad Boyd for eight yards. After an incomplete pass, a run missed the first down by inches, but on fourth down Chris Dantin got six yards.

With time running out, Jones threw to Keigley again, but the Rebs kept him from getting out of bounds at the 20. LSU used its last timeout with only ten seconds left to play. Huddling with his quarterback, Coach Charlie McClendon told him what play to run and then said, "Bert, this is what you came to LSU for." "You know what [Jones] did?" the coach told reporters after the game. "He winked at me! Can you believe that? He winked at me."

Jones' pass for Keigley was incomplete, but the Tigers caught a

TIGERS

break when the Rebels were flagged for interference. First down at the ten, four seconds to go. A pass in the end zone was batted away; the clock rolled to one second.

The scoreboard horn was already sounding when Jones' pass hit tailback Brad Davis at the one; he spun backwards into the end zone. Rusty Jackson stayed calm under pressure -- as Jones had done -- and booted the game-winning PAT.

You live every day with pressure. As Elijah did so long ago and as Bert Jones did against Ole Miss, you lay it on the line with everybody watching. Your family, coworkers, or employees – they depend on you. You know the pressure of a deadline, of a job evaluation, of taking the risk of asking someone to go out with you, of driving in rush-hour traffic.

Help in dealing with daily pressure is readily available, and the only price you pay for it is your willingness to believe. God will give you the grace to persevere if you ask prayerfully.

And while you may need some convincing, the pressures of daily living are really small potatoes since they all will pass. The real pressure comes when you stare into the face of eternity because what you do with it is irrevocable and forever. You can handle that pressure easily enough by deciding for Jesus. Eternity is then taken care of; the pressure's off – forever.

When you're standing back there with the ball and you're six points down and the horn is blowing -- that's pressure.
-- Charlie McCendon on Bert Jones' last-second TD pass

The greatest pressure you face in life
concerns where you will spend eternity,
which can be dealt with by deciding for Jesus.

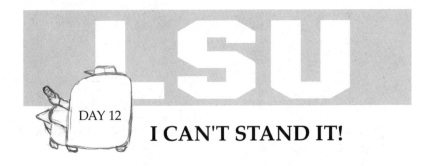

I CAN'T STAND IT!

Read Exodus 32:1-20.

"[Moses'] anger burned and he threw the tablets out of his hands, breaking them to pieces at the foot of the mountain" (v. 19).

The player who would become what Coach Dale Brown called the best captain he ever had at LSU was so frustrated because he wasn't playing that he was exploring the options available to him if he transferred.

As the 1985-86 season neared, sophomore Ricky Blanton "didn't figure into LSU's plans" and Blanton knew it. He had averaged only 3.5 points and 1.8 rebounds in limited playing time as a freshman, and Blanton had pretty much decided LSU didn't figure into his plans either.

The stark truth was that when Blanton arrived at LSU from Miami, where he had been the prep player of the year, "he was suddenly in over his head talent-wise." The Tigers were loaded with future NBA players like John Williams, Jerry Reynolds, and Nikita Wilson. Blanton didn't stand much of a chance.

But he wanted to play, not sit on the bench as part of a great team. He had been recruited by Miami, Michigan, Missouri, and FSU, so he considered transferring. "I think every freshman experiences the frustration of not playing as much as they're used to," he explained. Ultimately, though, Blanton decided to stay. "I think I made a wise move," he said. And how.

As it turned out, LSU needed help at center that season, and Blanton made the position change from small forward. At 6-6, he couldn't even dunk the ball, but he hit the weights and bulked up. Late in the season, he became a starter, and the Tigers soared all the way to the Final Four.

Before he left, Blanton was team captain and twice All-SEC, his frustration over limited playing time a faint memory.

The traffic light catches you when you're running late for work or your doctor's appointment. The bureaucrat gives you red tape when you want assistance. Your daughter refuses to take her homework seriously. Makes your blood boil, doesn't it?

Frustration is part of God's testing ground that is life even if much of what frustrates us today results from man-made organizations, bureaucracies, and machines. What's important is not that you encounter frustration—that's a given—but how you handle it. Do you respond with curses, screams, and violence? Or with a deep breath, a silent prayer, and calm persistence, and patience?

It may be difficult to imagine Jesus stuck in traffic or waiting for hours in a long line in a government office. It is not difficult, however, to imagine how he would act in such situations, and, thus, to know exactly how you should respond. No matter how frustrated you are.

A life of frustration is inevitable for any coach whose main enjoyment is winning.

-- *NFL Hall of Fame coach Chuck Noll*

**Frustration is a vexing part of life,
but God expects us to handle it gracefully.**

IN GOD'S OWN TIME

Read James 5:7-12.

"Be patient, then, brothers, until the Lord's coming" (v. 7).

Tom Petty once crooned, "The waiting is the hardest part." For the 2007 Tigers, the words rang true as they impatiently waited to hear whether or not they would be playing Ohio State for the national championship.

"Everybody counted us out after we lost to Arkansas," quarterback Matt Flynn said. It certainly looked that way after the Tigers tumbled to No. 7 in the BCS standings following the defeat. But the Tigers rallied to whip Tennessee 21-14 to win the SEC.

On the charter flight home from Atlanta, the captain gave them updates on scores. "He kept coming on and telling us the score of the West Virginia game," Flynn remembered. West Virginia was No. 2, and Pitt pulled the upset 13-9. "Then he told us the Oklahoma score in the fourth quarter." The Sooners clobbered top-ranked Missouri 38-17.

So when the Tigers hit the ground, hurried to the phones, and got the official final scores, they had an inkling that they had a chance. "When I heard [the two scores]," defensive back and team captain Craig Steltz said, "I thought 'We've got a shot.'"

They still had to wait, though, until the next night for the official annoucement on a 7 p.m. television show. All-American defensive tackle Glenn Dorsey said he spent Sunday trying to

TIGERS

avoid thinking about what they would or would not hear that evening. "I didn't want to get all excited and have a big letdown," Dorsey said. Flynn said, "I tried all day not to think about it, not to get my hopes up."

LSU officials learned the good news before the TV show and purposely didn't tell the players. Finally, at 7:21 p.m., the LSU players erupted in celebration when they heard what they had so impatiently been waiting for: They were in the big game.

Have you ever left a restaurant because the server didn't take your order quickly enough? Complained at your doctor's office about how long you had to wait? Wondered how much longer a sermon was going to last?

It isn't just the machinations of the world with which we're impatient; we want God to move at our pace, not his. For instance, how often have you prayed and expected – indeed, demanded – an immediate answer from God? And aren't Christians the world over impatient for the glorious day when Jesus will return and set everything right? We're in a hurry but God obviously isn't.

As rare as it seems to be, patience is nevertheless included among the likes of gentleness, humility, kindness, and compassion as attributes of a Christian.

God expects us to be patient. He knows what he's doing, he is in control, and his will shall be done. On his schedule, not ours.

It seemed like it took forever to announce who was going to play.
-- Glenn Dorsey

God moves in his own time, so often we must wait for him to act, remaining faithful and patient.

DAY 14

BE PREPARED

Read Matthew 10:5-23.

"I am sending you out like sheep among wolves. Therefore
be as shrewd as snakes and as innocent as doves" (v. 16).

For the fans, the Tigers whipped top-ranked Florida on the field
Saturday, Oct. 11, 1997. For the team, though, the game was won
in the meeting rooms in the days leading up to the game.

Before that exciting night, the Tigers had played football for
more than a century and had never beaten a top-ranked opponent;
they were 0-7-1. This night was LSU's though; in 93 fourth-quarter
seconds, the Tigers broke a 14-14 tie with a pair of touchdowns.
Cedrick Donaldson returned his second interception of the night
31 yards for a score with 11:40 left. LSU then scored four plays
after the Gators fumbled the ensuing kickoff with quarterback
Herb Tyler going twelve yards on the option. The points held up
as LSU won 28-21.

The upset win over the defending national champions was no
fluke. Rather, it was the result of careful planning and preparation
by Coach Gerry DiNardo and his staff. They came up with what
was called "a masterful game plan" that was executed "almost
flawlessly" by Tyler and his offense and a scrambling defense.

On offense, DiNardo decided to "smack Florida in the mouth,"
by attacking in the middle. The Tigers "put in two simple power
plays: a new trap and a new belly play." "It worked. LSU rushed
38 times for 158 yards with Kevin Faulk gaining 78 yards and full-

TIGERS

back Tommy Banks carrying five times for 34 yards and a score.

On defense, the Tigers kept the starters fresh by constantly working in line and linebacker reserves. This worked, too, for five sacks and four interceptions. Florida had only 49 yards rushing.

The Tigers were prepared, and the result was a historic win.

You know the importance of preparation in your own life. You went to the bank for a car loan, facts and figures in hand. That presentation you made at work was seamless because you practiced. The kids' school play suffered no meltdowns because they rehearsed. Knowing what you need to do and doing what you must to succeed isn't luck; it's preparation.

Jesus understood this, and he prepared his followers by lecturing them and by sending them on field trips. Two thousand years later, the life of faith requires similar training and study. You prepare so you'll be ready when that unsaved neighbor standing beside you at your backyard grill asks about Jesus. You prepare so you will know how God wants you to live. You prepare so you are certain in what you believe when the secular, godless world challenges it.

And one day you'll see God face to face. You certainly want to be prepared for that.

We won that game during the week. We were prepared, and we were ready.
            -- LSU quarterback Herb Tyler on the win over No. 1 Florida

**Living in faith requires constant study
and training, preparation for the day
when you meet God face to face.**

CHEAP TRICKS

Read Acts 19:11-20.

"The evil spirit answered them, 'Jesus I know, and I know about Paul, but who are you?'" (v. 15)

The Tigers once pulled off a trick play so daring that it could persuasively be argued that no coach in his right mind would try it today.

LSU's 1935 football team went 9-1, a record topped to that point only by the sensational 10-0 team of 1908. The squad lost the opener to Rice 10-7 and then ripped off nine straight wins. In fact, the Tigers would not lose another regular-season game until the middle of the 1937 season.

The star of the team was end Gaynell Tinsley, LSU's first consensus All-America (twice), a member of the College Football Hall of Fame, and the only player named unanimously to the Early Years Team of the Century. He was head coach from 1948-54.

Both the 1935 and '36 teams went undefeated in the SEC to win the league championship. After conference wins over Vanderbilt, Auburn, and Miss. State, the '35 Tigers had a showdown with Georgia on Nov. 16 in Athens. LSU won 13-0 behind halfback Bill Crass, who had a 23-yard touchdown run.

One particular play had everyone buzzing, though, as the Tigers used some bold trickery to notch their first score. LSU was backed up to its own four-yard line and lined up to punt with Abe Mickal (See Devotion No. 65.) standing deep in the end zone to kick.

He got a good snap, stepped forward, and swung his foot. Instead of kicking, though, he handed the ball behind his back to fellow halfback Jesse Fatherree. Described as "a fine runner and one of the school's all-time best defensive backs," Fatherree took off down the left sideline -- and kept going. And kept going.

He covered 106 yards, all the way to the Bulldog goal, some major "trickeration" that caught Georgia flat-footed.

Scam artists are everywhere — and they love trick plays. An e-mail encourages you to send money to some foreign country to get rich. That guy at your front door offers to resurface your driveway at a ridiculously low price. A TV ad promises a pill to help you lose weight without diet or exercise.

You've been around; you check things out before deciding. The same approach is necessary with spiritual matters, too, because false religions and bogus Christian denominations abound. The key is what any group does with Jesus. Is he the son of God, the ruler of the universe, and the only way to salvation? If not, then what the group espouses is something other than the true Word of God.

The good news about Jesus does indeed sound too good to be true. But the only catch is that there is no catch. No trick -- just the truth.

When you run trick plays and they work, you're a genius. But when they don't work, folks question your sanity.

-- Bobby Bowden

God's promises through Jesus sound too good to be true, but the only catch is that there is no catch.

DRESSED FOR SUCCESS

Read Galatians 5:16-26.

"So I say, live by the Spirit. . . . The sinful nature desires
what is contrary to the Spirit. . . . The acts of the sinful
nature are obvious: . . . I warn you, as I did before, that
those who live like this will not inherit the kingdom of
God" (vv. 16, 17, 19, 21).

The most successful program in NCAA women's track and field history pulled off a breathtaking comeback in 2008 to win yet another national championship.

Through 2009, the LSU women have won a staggering 25 national championships. Between 1987 and 1997, they won eleven consecutive outdoor national championships, "a streak that stands as the benchmark of excellence in women's collegiate athletics to this day."

On the last day of the 2008 outdoor championships, however, coach Dennis Shaver's women were in a deep hole, trailing front-running Arizona State 59-31. That's when they pulled off a furious comeback -- in the space of 34 minutes.

LaTavia Thomas finished second in the 800 meters; Kelly Baptiste and Samantha Henry went four-five in the 200. Nickiesha Wilson, who had won the 400-meter hurdles the night before, finished second in the 100 hurdles with Jessica Ohanaja finishing sixth. Almost before anybody had time to count the points, the Lady Tigers had tied the Sun Devils -- with one event left.

TIGERS

All the LSU women had to do was finish ahead of Arizona State in the 1600-meter relay. The team of Brooklynn Morris, Baptiste (a late replacement for Wilson, who had a sore hamstring), Thomas, and Deonna Lawrence ran to glory, finishing in second place, ahead of the fifth-place Sun Devils.

The poster women for collegiate track and field success were on top again.

Are you a successful person? Your answer, of course, depends upon how you define success. Is the measure of your success based on the number of digits in your bank balance, the square footage of your house, that title on your office door, the size of your boat?

Certainly the world determines success by wealth, fame, prestige, awards, and possessions. Our culture screams that life is all about gratifying your own needs and wants. If it feels good, do it. It's basically the Beach Boys' philosophy of life.

But all success of this type has one glaring shortcoming: You can't take it with you. Eventually, Daddy takes the T-bird away. Like life itself, all these things are fleeting.

A more lasting way to approach success is through the spiritual rather than the physical. The goal becomes not money or backslaps by sycophants but eternal life spent with God. Success of that kind is forever.

Success demands singleness of purpose.

-- Vince Lombardi

Success isn't permanent, and failure isn't fatal -- unless you're talking about your relationship with God.

NAME DROPPING

Read Exodus 3:13-20.

"God said to Moses, 'I AM WHO I AM. This is what you are to say to the Israelites: 'I AM has sent me to you'"" (v. 14).

More than fifty years after their appearance as a crucial part of the 1958 national championship team, they remain the most legendary -- almost mythological -- group of reserves in the history of college football. They were the Chinese Bandits.

A rule change in 1958 limiting substitutions benefited LSU, which had questionable depth. Coach Paul Dietzel divided his squad into three teams: the White team, his best athletes who played both ways; the Go Team, a group of offensive specialists; and the Chinese Bandits, the defensive team.

The Bandits comprised LSU's second best linemen and third-string backs. They became national celebrities after the Alabama game when Dietzel put this team of subs into the game with the Tide sitting at the LSU five. "It took guts," assistant coach Charlie McClendon said about taking out Billy Cannon and the other best players and putting in a whole team of subs in a scoreless game.

The Bandits held Alabama to one yard on three plays, and a legend was born. They became a national phenomenon. When *Life* magazine did a spread on the Bayou Bengals, they didn't feature Cannon or Dietzel; they focused on the Bandits.

They weren't just reputation. In an astounding statistic, they limited opponents to 0.9 yards per play for the season.

How did the nickname arise? Dietzel got the idea when he was coaching at the University of Cincinnati. His favorite cartoon strip was "Terry and the Pirates," which was set in the Orient. A character named Chopsticks Joe once said, "Chinese bandits are the most vicious people on earth." Dietzel never forgot it.

Nicknames such as the Chinese Bandits are not slapped haphazardly upon individuals but rather reflect widely held perceptions about the person named. Proper names do that also.

Nowhere throughout history has this concept been more prevalent that in the Bible, where a name is not a mere label but is an expression of the essential nature of the named one. That is, a person's name reveals his or her character. Even God shares this concept; to know the name of God is to know God as he has chosen to reveal himself to us.

What does your name say about you? Honest, trustworthy, a seeker of the truth and a person of God? Or does the mention of your name cause your coworkers to whisper snide remarks, your neighbors to roll their eyes, or your friends to start making allowances for you?

Most importantly, what does your name say about you to God? He, too, knows you by name.

The greatest thrill I ever had in athletics was the opportunity to be associated with the Bandits.

-- Paul Dietzel

Live so that your name evokes positive associations by people you know, by the public, and by God.

MEMORY LOSS

Read 1 Corinthians 11:17-29.

"[D]o this in remembrance of me" (v. 24).

The record book says she is the greatest player in LSU women's basketball history, but only the most avid Lady Tiger fans might be able to remember her today.

The first of LSU's great teams was the 1976-77 squad, the only Lady Tigers to reach the national championship game of a post-season tournament. The BenGals, as they were known then, went 29-8, but that sterling slate was eclipsed by the 1977-78 team, which set a school record for wins with an incredible 37-3 record.

Both teams were led by a dominant 6-2 center from Australia named Maree Jackson whose two seasons at LSU almost defy belief. Her 1,021 points and 539 rebounds in 1978-79 remain to this day the most in LSU and SEC history for a season. Her freshman year she set the school record by averaging 27.7 points per game. Her career average of 26.4 points per game is still the school and the SEC record. (All her conference records carry an asterisk since the SEC did not sponsor women's basketball until 1982-83.)

Jackson twice set the school record with 27 rebounds in a game. Her 539 rebounds in 1977-78 and 493 the following season are still the two best seasons in Lady Tiger history. She set the LSU records with 19 field goals in a game and 409 for a season. She was also the most accurate shooter in school and SEC history with a career field-goal percentage of 65.1.

TIGERS

Jackson was tough too. When the Lady Tigers met heavily favored Immaculata in the semifinals of the 1977 AIAW National Tournament, she had recently undergone root canal surgery. She played anyhow, finishing with 29 points and 19 rebounds to lead the Bengals to the 74-68 upset and into the finals.

But Maree Jackson played in the days before the SEC, the NCAA championship, ESPN, and televised games, so her accomplishments remain part of a dimly remembered distant past.

Memory makes us who we are. Whether our memories are dreams or nightmares, they shape us and to a large extent determine our actions and reactions. Alzheimer's is so terrifying because it steals our memory from us and in the process we lose ourselves. We disappear.

The greatest tragedy of our lives is that God remembers. In response to that memory, he condemns us for our sin. On the other hand, the greatest joy of our lives is that God remembers. In response to that memory, he came as Jesus to wash even the memory of our sins away.

Through memory, we encounter revival. At the Last Supper, Jesus instructed his disciples and us to remember. In sharing this unique meal with fellow believers and remembering Jesus and his actions, we meet Christ again not just as a memory but as an actual living presence. To remember is to keep our faith alive.

I don't want them to forget Babe Ruth. I just want them to remember Hank Aaron.

-- *Hank Aaron*

We remember Jesus,
and God will not remember our sins.

DAY 19

RUN FOR IT

Read John 20:1-10.

"Peter and the other disciple started for the tomb. Both were running, but the other disciple outran Peter and reached the tomb first" (vv. 3-4).

His career as an LSU running back started out so badly that his coach had to tell him repeatedly that things would get better. And, oh, yes, they did.

Charles Alexander ranks right there with the greatest running backs in Tiger football history. From 1975-78, Alexander was one of the most durable and successful backs in the game. He was first-team All-America and All-SEC in both 1977 and 1978 and the SEC's Most Valuable Player in 1977. He set nine SEC records and 27 LSU records, including most rushing yards in a single game (237), touchdowns in a season, and yards rushing in a season (1,686). In 1989, Alexander was inducted into the LSU Athletic Hall of Fame.

All of that fame and success looked like an impossible dream, however, after the way Alexander's career started. In his first varsity game, the season opener against Nebraska in 1975, he carried the ball eight times for minus-two yards. Head coach Charles McClendon recalled that in the dressing room after the game, he patted Alexander on the back and encouraged him by promising, "Charlie, things are going to get better." McClendon said the downcast freshman just looked at him "and didn't say a word."

TIGERS

Well, things got better in the next game, but not by much. Against Texas A&M, Alexander carried eight times for a rousing three yards. Again, McClendon had to tell a dejected Alexander that things would get better. At that point, the stat sheet was pretty pitiful: Alexander had sixteen carries for one yard.

But McClendon was right. Things got better as Alexander ran to glory, a pro career, and the nickname "Alexander the Great."

Hit the ground running -- every morning that's what you do as you leave the house and re-enter the rat race. You run errands, you run though a presentation; you give someone a run for his money; you always want to be in the running and never run-of-the-mill.

You're always running toward something, such as your goals, or away from something, such as your past. Many of us spend much of our lives foolhardily attempting to run away from God, the purposes he has for us, and the blessings he is waiting to give us.

No matter how hard or how far you run, though, you can never outrun yourself or God. God keeps pace with you, calling you in the short run to take care of the long run by falling to your knees and running for your life -- to Jesus -- just as Peter and the other disciple ran that first Easter morning.

On your knees, you run all the way to glory.

Not many backs can take the pounding Charlie Alexander takes 20, 30, 40 times a game and still come back ready to do it again.
-- Former Tulane assistant coach Vic Eumont

You can run to eternity by going to your knees.

THE HEALING TOUCH

Read Matthew 17:14-20.

"If you have faith as small as a mustard seed, you can say to this mountain, 'Move from here to there' and it will move. Nothing will be impossible for you" (v. 20).

For two years, Jarvis Green played football in such constant and debilitating pain that he couldn't even tie his shoes. He couldn't get rid of the pain either -- until one night he prayed.

In 1998, Green, a defensive end, set an LSU freshman record with eight sacks. As a sophomore he had seven sacks and 51 tackles. All the while, he was in agony with a bad back.

"It was killing me," he said. "I couldn't tie my shoes. I had to lay in the bed to do everything, including putting my shoes on." The pain was so bad that he had to tell people he wasn't handicapped, and he quit going home to avoid questions from family, friends, and neighbors, who would lovingly volunteer to help him with the slightest physical chores.

The pain resulted from a minor car accident that left Green with two fractured vertebrae and two bulging discs. He played through the pain, but it kept getting worse. At the last scrimmage of the 2000 preseason, it was obvious the pain had become so extreme it would limit Green's playing time.

And then God stepped in. That night, Green prayed for about thirty minutes for relief. When he awoke the next morning, he discovered he could move around without pain. In his excitement, he flapped his arms, jumped on the bed, and hit the wall so vehemently that he woke his roommate up. And he did it all without pain.

"As the season went on," Green said, "I was scared [the pain] might come up again. But it never did." God had taken it away for good, and Green went on to a pro career.

If we believe in miraculous healing at all, we have pretty much come to consider it to be a relatively rare occurrence. All too often, when we are ill or hurting, our path to a cure parallels that of Jarvis Green: 1) call a doctor; 2) try therapy or take pills; 3) pray when nothing else works. Even if we are people of strong faith, we tend to rely on heavy-duty earthmoving equipment rather than prayer to move a mountain.

The truth is, though, that divine healing occurs with quite astonishing regularity; the problem is our perspective. We are usually quite effusive in our thanks to and praise for a doctor or a particular medicine without considering that God is the one responsible for all healing.

We should remember also that "natural" healing occurs because our bodies react as God created them to. Those healings, too, are divine; they, too, are miraculous. Faith healing is really nothing more – or less – than giving credit where credit is due.

The last two years I was up and down, but I was pain-free, and I thank God for that.

-- Jarvis Green

**God does in fact heal continuously everywhere;
all too often we just don't notice.**

CHANCE MEETING

Read Luke 24:13-35.

"That same day two of them were going to a village. . . .
They were talking with each other about everything that
had happened. . . . Jesus himself came up and walked
along with them" (vv. 13-15).

A chance meeting in another country ultimately resulted in LSU basketball history.

In 1986, LSU coach Dale Brown was on a European tour of coaching clinics. On a U.S. Army base in West Germany, Brown entertained a crowd by doing some tricks. He told everyone that simply by keeping your elbow straight, you could stand at one end of a basketball court, throw the ball the length of the court, and make at least three out of ten baskets. He then proceeded to do just exactly that: make three baskets.

In the crowd, a teenager "thought he was real funny," though he didn't really know much about Brown. "I remember they told me that the LSU basketball coach, Dale Brown, was coming," said the teen. "I thought to myself, 'Well, who's that?'" Impressed by Brown's tricks, the teen approached him and asked about improving his jumping ability. In turn impressed by the young man's 6'6" of height, Brown asked him what his rank was. "No rank," the youngster replied. "I'm 13 years old."

The teen was Shaquille O'Neal.

Brown's next question was, "Uh, your dad around?" Brown told

O'Neal he was going to keep in touch. O'Neal recalled, "I waited about a month and started thinking, 'He's not going to write to me.'" But when the family left West Germany and returned home to New Jersey, "there was a whole stack of letters from Coach Brown waiting for me at my grandmother's house. Altogether," O'Neal said, "I got about 2,000 letters from Coach Brown."

And what Coach Brown and LSU got from what began as a chance meeting was a basketball legend.

Maybe you met your spouse on a blind date or in Kroger's frozen food section. Perhaps a conversation in an elevator or over lunch led to a job offer.

Chance meetings often shape our lives. Some meetings, however, are too important to be left to what seem like the whims of life. If your child is sick, you don't wait until you happen to bump into a physician at Starbuck's to seek help.

So it is with Jesus. Too much is at stake to leave a meeting with him to chance. Instead, you intentionally seek him at church, in the pages of your Bible, on your knees in prayer, or through a conversation with a friend or neighbor. How you conduct the search doesn't matter; what matters is that you find him.

Once you've met him, you should then intentionally cultivate the acquaintance until it is a deep, abiding, life-shaping and life-changing friendship.

If you think it's hard to meet new people, try picking up the wrong golf ball.

-- *Jack Lemmon*

A meeting with Jesus should not be a chance encounter, but instead should be sought out.

WITNESS PROTECTION

Read Hebrews 11:39-12:2.

"Therefore, since we are surrounded by such a great cloud of witnesses, . . . let us run with perseverance the race marked out for us" (v. 12:1).

The toughest ticket in town is a ducat for an LSU football game. In 2008, though, the Tigers opened their season at home before such a small crowd that the stadium "seemed about half empty."

Much about the season opener against Appalachian State seemed normal. The student section was nearly full when the Golden Band from Tigerland performed its pregame show. The fans dutifully stood for the alma mater and the national anthem.

But the size of the crowd served notice that this was not an ordinary Saturday in Baton Rouge. That and a pregame intonation from the PA announcer: "Ladies and gentlemen, it's Saturday morning in Tiger Stadium."

The teams kicked off at 10:06 a.m., almost six hours before the originally scheduled 4 p.m. start. "It's the earliest kickoff I've ever had except when I was in the ninth grade," coach Les Miles said. "It felt like we were back at [preseason] camp," receiver Brandon LaFell remarked. The Tigers ate their pregame meal at 6:30 and were on the practice field at 9 a.m. "You got up, ate some grits and eggs and were ready to roll," said linebacker Darry Beckwith, adding, "I'm not a morning person."

So what was up with the abnormal starting time? Hurricane

Gustav, that's what. State officials had declared there would be an early kickoff or none at all.

Thus, the stadium was only about half full when the Tigers -- apparently not bothered by the early start or the small crowd -- jumped out to a 31-0 lead. From there, the crowd got even smaller as folks fled for the air conditioning and/or the shade.

You, too, probably don't have a huge crowd of folks applauding your efforts every day, and you certainly don't have TV cameras broadcasting your every move to an enthralled audience as the Tigers did even with that early start. Sometimes you may even feel alone. A child's illness, the slow death of a loved one, financial troubles, worries about your health – you feel isolated.

But a person of faith is never alone, and not just because you're aware of God's presence. You are always surrounded by a crowd of God's most faithful witnesses, those in the present and those from the past. Their faithfulness both encourages and inspires. They, too, have faced the difficult circumstances with which you contend, and they remained faithful and true to God.

With their examples before you, you can endure your trials, looking in hope and faithfulness beyond your immediate troubles to God's glorious future. Your final victory in Christ will be even sweeter because of your struggles.

A very small crowd here today. I can count the people on one hand. Can't be more than 30.

– Announcer Michael Abrahamson

The person of faith is surrounded by a crowd of witnesses whose faithfulness in difficult times inspires us to remain true to God no matter what.

LIMITED-TIME OFFER

Read Psalm 103.

*"As for man, his days are like grass, he flourishes like a
flower of the field; the wind blows over it and it is gone.
. . . But from everlasting to everlasting the Lord's love is
with those who fear him" (vv. 15-17).*

He exploded onto the scene, scoring three touchdowns in his
first game at LSU. That game, however, was to be his last. Within
a few months, he was dead of tuberculosis.

In the summer of 1931, Gov. Huey Long summoned LSU athletic
business manager Red Heard to the governor's mansion and
shoved a newspaper clipping into his face. It detailed the athletic
exploits of Art Foley of the New Mexico Military Institute.

Heard took a train for Foley's home in Oklahoma and found
him on vacation with his parents. "I knew nothing about the
boy's football ability other than what I had read, [but] on the golf
course he looked like a great athlete," Heard said. Heard played
golf with Foley every day for more than a week and received a
commitment from him to come play football for LSU in the fall.

Since he was a junior-college transfer, Foley was eligible for
LSU's first game, but a tooth infection sidelined him. On Oct. 3,
1931, in the second game of the season, Foley made his debut
against Spring Hill in the first night football game ever played in
Baton Rouge.

Foley was dazzling. His three touchdowns included a 56-yard

TIGERS

run from scrimmage and a 62-yard punt return. LSU won easily 35-0, and both Long and head coach Russ Cohen were ecstatic.

But then only a few days after the game, Foley began to hemorrhage in the shower. A specialist diagnosed tuberculosis and advised Foley to return home where the dryer climate might hasten his recovery.

He died within a few months. Long broke down and cried when Heard told him the news.

A heart attack, cancer, or an accident will probably take -- or has already taken -- someone you know or love such as Art Foley who is "too young to die."

The death of a younger person never seems to "make sense." That's because such a death belies the common view of death as the natural end of a life lived well and lived long. Moreover, you can't see the whole picture as God does, so you can't know how the death furthers God's kingdom.

At such a time, you can seize the comforting truth that God is in control and therefore everything will be all right one day. You can also gain a sense of urgency in your own life by appreciating that God's offer of life through Jesus Christ is a limited-time offer that expires at your death – and there's no guarantee about when that will be.

No one knows when he is going to die, so if we're going to accept Christ, we'd better not wait because death might come in the blink of an eye.
-- Bobby Bowden

**God offers you life through Jesus Christ,
but you must accept it before your death,
which is when the offer expires.**

TEN TO REMEMBER

Read Exodus 20:1-17.

"God spoke all these words: 'I am the Lord your God . . . .
You shall have no other gods before me'" (vv. 1, 3).

Tigerland's resident expert on great plays, Billy Cannon, agreed: Warren Morris' home run to beat Miami in the 1996 College World Series is the most exciting moment in LSU athletic history.

"That's No. 1 because it won a national championship," Cannon said. It was also No. 1 on a list drawn up by *Advocate* sportswriter Glenn Guilbeau of the "ten most memorable and significant games in the Skip Bertman era." Bertman won 870 games, seven SEC championships, and five national championships as LSU's head baseball coach from 1984-2001.

No. 2 on the list is the 6-5 win over Stanford that won the 2000 national championship in the bottom of the ninth. (See Devotion No. 60.) No. 3 is the 6-3 win over Wichita State in 1991 that won LSU's first national title.

No. 4 is the 5-4 win over Texas A&M in 1989 to win the NCAA Central Regional title. The Aggies were ranked No. 1 and were playing in their own park, but LSU beat them twice in one day.

No. 5 is the 7-6 win over South Carolina in 1990 that won the South I Regional. No. 6 is the 14-7 win over Long Beach State in 11 innings in 1997 that won a regional. Eddy Furniss tied the game in the eighth with a solo home run before the seven-run outburst.

The seventh most significant win is the 6-5 won over Long

TIGERS

Beach State in 1993 that propelled LSU to the title game. The Tigers trailed 5-3 in the bottom of the ninth. Armando Rios tied it with a double and scored on Todd Walker's one-out single.

No. 8 is the 13-11 win over Cal State Fullerton in 1998 that won a regional. LSU trailed early 7-0. No. 9 is the 8-0 romp past Wichita State in 1993 that won the national title. No. 10 is the 1997 13-6 blowout of Alabama for the repeat national title.

For LSU fans, this list is indeed ten to remember for the ages.

You've got your list and you're ready to go: a gallon of paint and a water hose from the hardware store; chips, peanuts, and sodas from the grocery store for watching tonight's football game with your buddies; the tickets for the band concert. Your list helps you remember.

God also made a list once of things he wanted you to remember; it's called the Ten Commandments. Just as your list reminds you to do something, so does God's list remind you of how you are to act in your dealings with other people and with him. A life dedicated to Jesus is a life devoted to relationships, and God's list emphasizes that the social life and the spiritual life of the faithful cannot be sundered. God's relationship to you is one of unceasing, unqualified love, and you are to mirror that divine love in your relationships with others. In case you forget, you have a list.

Society today treats the Ten Commandments as if they were the ten suggestions. Never compromise on right or wrong.
-- College baseball coach Gordie Gillespie

God's list is a set of instructions on how you are to conduct yourself with other people and with him.

WINNING

Read 1 John 5:1-12.

"Who is it that overcomes the world? Only he who believes that Jesus is the Son of God" (v. 5).

Baton Rouge Wins Without Winning." So did a newspaper once describe an LSU win.

The Tigers had their most successful football season yet in 1896, a time when LSU advertised that "it offered six courses of study, had buildings lighted by electricity, free tuition, and a total cost of $138 for the full nine-month session to cover 'room, board, washing, fuel, lights and medical attendance.'" As the paper headline indicates, the Tulane win that season was claimed in rather unusual fashion. LSU started off with a 40-0 shellacking of Centenary; then came the third-ever meeting with Tulane.

Tulane led 2-0 on a safety in the last half when a player was injured. After a Tulane substitute ran onto the field to take his place, the LSU captain, Edwin A. Scott, protested to the referee that the new guy was an illegal player. LSU's position was that prior to the game the two schools had agreed that students who had not yet entered graduate school at Tulane had to sign an affidavit that they planned to enter before they could play in the game. The player in dispute refused to sign that affidavit.

The referee, a Lt. Wall, who apparently was a military instructor at LSU, agreed with LSU. When the Tulane captain refused to order the player out of the game, Wall ruled that Tulane had

TIGERS

forfeited the game by refusing to play without him.

This decision "brought a wild yell from the Baton Rouge fellows" but apparently fans of both teams were unhappy. Said the newspaper, "There wasn't a rooter on the ground who wasn't mad at the interruption of the sport." Wall fixed the final score of the game LSU "won without winning" at 6-0.

Life itself, not just athletic events such as LSU football games, is a competition. You vie against all the other job or college applicants. You compete against others for a date. Sibling rivalry is real; just ask your brother or sister.

Inherent in any competition or any situation in which you strive to win is the involvement of an antagonist. You always have an opponent to overcome, even if it's an inanimate video game, a golf course, or even yourself.

Nobody wants to be numbered among life's losers. We recognize them when we see them, and maybe mutter a prayer that says something like, "There but for the grace of God go I."

But one adversary will defeat us: Death will claim us all. We can turn the tables on this foe, though; we can defeat the grave. A victory is possible, however, only through faith in Jesus Christ. With Jesus, we have hope beyond death because we have life.

With Jesus, we win. For all of eternity.

LSU can't have a losing football team because that will mean that I am associated with a loser.

-- *Louisiana Governor Huey Long*

Death is the ultimate opponent;
Jesus is the ultimate victor.

NEVER TOO LATE

Read Genesis 21:1-7.

"And [Sarah] added, 'Who would have said to Abraham that Sarah would nurse children? Yet I have borne him a son in his old age'" (v. 7).

Time was running out on the Lady Tigers' season, and they didn't look like they were going to do anything about it.

"Frustrating" and "embarrassing" was the way one writer described how LSU played in the first half against Louisiana Tech in the semifinals of the 2003 NCAA West Regional. The Lady Tigers trailed 33-23 at the half and "looked bad doing it. . . . LSU was floundering and frustrated. Rebounds were something the Lady Tigers read about in history class. A second-chance basket was an extinct species." The cynics had said that LSU (29-3) would be the first No. 1 seed to fall. They were grinning.

So after Coach Sue Gunter blistered her team at halftime, they came out and blew Tech off the court, right? Nope. Tech scored the half's first five points and went on to lead 50-33 with fourteen minutes to play. It was getting late.

Not too late, though. Center Aiysha Smith got some momentum going when she hit a three and a short jumper, "a volcanic eruption of scoring by LSU's standards to that point." But that seemed to jump-start the rest of the team, especially freshman Seimone Augustus, who scored ten points in the last half. Before the dust settled, the Lady Tigers had run off sixteen straight points.

TIGERS

When Doneeka Hodges hit a jumper in the lane with 5:23 left, the run was 24-6 and LSU had its first lead of the game at 57-56. DeTrina White's basket from the right baseline made it a 28-7 surge and a four-point lead. When the scoreboard ran out of time, LSU had a 69-63 win by outscoring Tech 36-13 to close the game.

Gunter admitted that in her more than forty years of playing and coaching, she had never seen such a big comeback in such a big game. It was just never too late for the Lady Tigers.

Getting that college degree. Getting married. Starting a new career. Though we may make all kinds of excuses, it's often never too late for life-changing decisions and milestones.

This is especially true in our faith life, which is based on God's promises. Abraham was 100 and Sarah was 90 when their first child was born. They were old folks even by the Bible's standards at the dawn of history. But God had promised them a child and just as God always does, he kept his promise no matter how unlikely it seemed.

God has made us all a promise of new life and hope through Jesus Christ. At any time in our lives – today even -- we can regret the things we have done wrong and the way we have lived, ask God in Jesus' name to forgive us for them, and discover a new way of living – forever.

It's never too late to change. God promised.

It's never too late to achieve success in sports.
-- Brooke de Lench, writer and lecturer on children and sports

**It's never too late to change a life
by turning it over to Jesus.**

DAY 27

FAMILY TIES

Read Mark 3:31-35.

"[Jesus] said, 'Here are my mother and my brothers! Whoever does God's will is my brother and sister and mother'" (vv. 34-35).

Todd Kinchen was born to play football for the Tigers. After all, it was what his family did.

His father, Gaynell "Gus" Kinchen, was named for Gaynell "Gus" Tinsley, LSU's first All-America (See Devotion No. 15.). The senior Kinchen was a Chinese Bandit from 1958-60 and made some of the biggest defensive plays of the era. Todd's uncle, Gary, played center for the Tigers from 1960-62. Todd's brother, Brian, was an All-SEC tight end who caught the game-winning touchdown from Tommy Hodson in 1987's 26-23 win over Georgia.

Todd's mother, Toni, was an LSU cheerleader for four years and twice was the homecoming queen. The school changed the rules after her reign to limit coeds to one stint as the queen. "I was hearing about LSU football as long as I can remember, since I was a child," Todd said. "Our family was such a part of it."

In 1990, though, he entered his name into the family journal of LSU football lore in a game against 11th-ranked Texas A&M. The week before, the Tigers had lost to Vanderbilt after Todd's game-winning touchdown catch was nullified by a penalty. "That was a disappointment," he recalled. "I just dedicated the A&M game to the Lord, and I think He blessed me."

TIGERS

Indeed. Todd had a game LSU associate athletic director Herb Vincent called "as spectacular a performance as anyone ever turned in around here." In a span of 1:23 of the fourth quarter, the junior split end and kick returner had a pair of "dazzling dashes" that ignited a 17-8 upset. He turned a short pass into a 79-yard touchdown and seconds later returned a punt 60 yards to set up a second touchdown.

But he was just doing what the Kinchen family always did.

Some wit said families are like fudge, mostly sweet with a few nuts. You can probably call the names of your sweetest relatives, whom you cherish, and of the nutty ones too, whom you mostly try to avoid at a family reunion.

Like it or not, you have a family, and that's God's doing. God cherishes the family so much that he chose to live in one as a son, a brother, and a cousin.

One of Jesus' more unsettling actions was to redefine the family. No longer is it a single household of blood relatives or even a clan or a tribe. Jesus' family is the result not of an accident of birth but rather a conscious choice. All those who do God's will are members of Jesus' family.

What a startling and wonderful thought! You have family members out there you don't even know who stand ready to love you just because you're part of God's family.

For Todd, playing for LSU was like stepping into the huge Bayou Bengal footprints of the Kinchens who had gone before him.
-- Sportswriter/Reporter Marty Mule

For followers of Jesus, family comes not from a shared ancestry but from a shared faith.

IN THE KNOW

Read John 4:19-26, 39-42.

"They said to the woman, . . . 'Now we have heard for ourselves, and we know that this man really is the Savior of the world'" (v. 42).

On a day when everybody claimed they knew something -- which they didn't -- one LSU player did know something. The result was the championship of the SEC, which made possible the national title.

On Dec. 1, 2007, the Tigers met Tennessee in the SEC's title game. The pre-game hoopla centered on Coach Les Miles rather than on what promised to be a thrilling contest. On the morning of the game, ESPN reported as fact that Miles -- a former Michigan player and assistant coach under Bo Schembechler -- would be taking over as the head coach of the Wolverines.

That prompted Miles to hold a press conference to declare that ESPN didn't know what it was talking about. "I'm the head coach at LSU. I will be the head coach at LSU," Miles stated. "I have no interest in talking to anyone else."

History subsequently revealed that Miles was indeed the only one around that day who really knew what was going on.

Except -- later on -- for LSU cornerback Jonathan Zenon.

Attention eventually shifted to the game, which saw Tennessee lead 14-13 with less than ten minutes left to play. The Vols lined up facing third and five from their own 14. Their formation had

TIGERS

Zenon "salivating" because he knew what was coming.

The Tennessee quarterback sailed a flat pass toward the wide receiver on Zenon's side. Zenon cut in front of the Volunteer, snagged the interception, and waltzed into the end zone. Ryan Perrilloux's run added the two-point conversion, and the final score of 21-14 was on the board.

The day started out with a bunch of folks not in the know at all and ended with a lone LSU player knowing exactly what he needed to.

Jonathan Zenon just knew what Tennessee would do in the same way you know certain things in your life. That your spouse loves you, for instance. That you are good at your job. That tea should be iced and sweetened. That a bad day fishing is still better than a good day at work. That the best barbecue comes from a pig. You know these things though no mathematician or philosopher can prove any of this on paper.

It's the same way with faith in Jesus: You just know that he is God's son and the savior of the world. You know it in the same way that you know LSU is the only team worth pulling for: with every fiber of your being, with all your heart, your mind, and your soul.

You just know, and because you know him, Jesus knows you. And that is all you really need to know.

I knew exactly what they were going to run.
-- Jonathan Zenon on his game-winning interception

A life of faith is lived in certainty and conviction:
You just know you know.

IMPORTANT STUFF

Read Matthew 6:25-34.

*"Seek first his kingdom and his righteousness, and all
these things will be given to you as well" (v. 33).*

Basketball was the top priority for much of Pete Maravich's life
until he finally found what really mattered.

The LSU and basketball legend admitted he was "dedicated,
possessed, and obsessed" by basketball even as a child. When he
was 12, a reporter asked him what he wanted to do with his life,
and Maravich replied, "Play pro basketball, get a big diamond
ring, and make a million dollars."

He got all that. In his three years on the LSU varsity (1967-70)
in a day when freshmen were ineligible, Maravich averaged 44.2
points per game, an all-time NCAA record. He set 11 NCAA and
34 SEC records as well as every Tiger scoring record that can be
measured. He scored 3,667 points, which doesn't include the 741
his freshman year; he also didn't have the three-point line.

Maravich was the third player drafted by the NBA in 1970;
he made league history by signing a $1.9 million contract with
the Atlanta Hawks. He was a five-time NBA All-Star and led the
league in scoring in 1977.

He had it all -- or so it seemed. After he left pro basketball
in 1980, he admitted he was searching for "life." He tried yoga,
Hinduism, vegetarianism, and other assorted "isms" that failed
to fulfill him. "My life," he said, "had no meaning at all."

TIGERS

Maravich reached rock bottom and there he found the priority that had been missing for the first 35 years of his life. He found his peace in Jesus. He became a lay preacher, sharing his message that through Christ the man he had become in his late 30s was far more important than the alcoholic basketball player he had been.

Before he died in 1988 of a heart attack at age 40 while playing basketball, "Pistol" Pete Maravich found his true priority in life.

Basketball may not be the most important thing in your life, but you do have priorities. What is it that you would surrender only with your dying breath? Your family? Every dime you have? Your LSU season tickets?

What about God? Would you denounce your faith in Jesus Christ rather than lose your children? Or everything you own?

God doesn't force us to make such unspeakable choices; nevertheless, followers of Jesus Christ often become confused about their priorities because so much in our lives clamors for attention and time. It all seems so worthwhile.

But Jesus' instructions are unequivocal: Seek God first. Turn to him first for help, fill your thoughts with what he wants for you and your life, use God's character as revealed in Jesus as the pattern for everything you do, and serve and obey him in all matters, at all moments.

God – and God alone – is No. 1.

If you focus on yourself, all the lights fade away and you become a fleeting moment in life.

-- Pete Maravich

God should always be number one in our lives.

THE GREATEST

Read Mark 9:33-37.

"If anyone wants to be first, he must be the very last, and the servant of all" (v. 35).

Throughout LSU's long and storied football history, many plays have earned the right to be called "great." Only one, however, is without question "the greatest."

On Halloween night 1959, Billy Cannon treated LSU fans to the greatest trick ever played on Ole Miss. Both teams were undefeated; the defending national-champion Tigers were ranked No. 1, Ole Miss No. 3. Interestingly, with new and stronger flood-lights and 100 percent humidity, "the foggy field assumed an unearthly quality, . . . a perfect setting for a Halloween game."

For much of the game, Cannon was the goat. His first-quarter fumble set up a Rebel field goal, and that 3-0 score held up into the last quarter. LSU was on the ropes, "worn and beaten for the first time in 18 games."

But with ten minutes left, Ole Miss punted and Cannon made another mistake. "We had a rule of not handling kicks inside the 15," he recalled. But "it was getting late. I thought, 'If I see a chance I'm going to try to bring it back.'"

So Cannon broke Coach Paul Dietzel's rule by fielding the ball at the 11 "and started an incredible, absolutely unbelievable run to glory." He was hit almost right away but shook off the tackle. He broke two more tackles before he busted through "a Rebel mob" at the 25. By the time Cannon hit midfield, eight Ole Miss players had had a hand on him. He gave a hip to the last would-be tackler at midfield and sailed the rest of the way like a white-shirted ghost wearing jersey number 20."

Wendell Harris kicked the extra point that prevented a tie because in the last minute of the game, Ole Miss had a fourth down at the LSU two. Warren Rabb, also the starting quarterback, hit the ball carrier at the one, and Cannon finished him off. LSU took possession with 18 seconds left and won 7-3.

We all want to be the greatest. The goal for the Tigers and their fans every season is the national championship. The competition at work is to be the most productive sales person on the staff or the Teacher of the Year. In other words, we define being the greatest in terms of the struggle for personal success. It's nothing new; the disciples saw greatness in the same way.

As Jesus illustrated, though, greatness in the Kingdom of God has nothing to do with the world's understanding of success. Rather, the greatest are those who channel their ambition toward the furtherance of Christ's kingdom through love and service, rather than their own advancement, which is a complete reversal of status and values as the world sees them.

After all, who could be greater than the person who has Jesus for a brother and God for a father? And that's every one of us.

That was the greatest run I ever saw in football.
-- Paul Dietzel on Billy Cannon's Halloween punt return

**To be great for God has nothing to do
with personal advancement and everything to do
with the advancement of Christ's kingdom.**

FACING THE MUSIC

Read Psalm 98.

"Sing to the Lord a new song, for he has done marvelous things" (*v. 1*).

If it's game night at Tiger Stadium, then the noise is so intense that the "game is not merely seen. It is HEARD." The most raucous noisemakers of them all will be a group that dresses alike and is nationally recognized for its excellence: the LSU Tiger Band.

"The Golden Band from Tigerland" began in 1893 as a military band with eleven members, including its organizers, cadets Wylie M. Barrow and Ruffin G. Pleasant. By the turn of the century, the Cadet Band had become a marching unit that toured the state and made personal appearances.

The first major change in the band occurred in 1915 with the establishment of a music department at LSU and the requirement that all music class participants perform in the Military Band. Even with the move to the current campus site in the mid-1920s, the band's primary duties remained military in nature. It made its first halftime appearance at a football game in 1924.

In the 1930s, Gov. Huey Long took a personal interest in the band. His determination to make it one of nation's biggest and best resulted in the membership reaching 250. With Director Castro Carazo, Long co-wrote several of the band's signature songs, including "Touchdown for LSU."

During World War II, Director J.S. Fisher had to supplement the

TIGERS

all-male band with female members, paving the way for coeds to become musicians and not only drum majorettes.

When the band building burned to the ground in 1958, the band lost its uniforms and most of its instruments. Only a lone baritone horn and sixteen sousaphones survived; the band still uses the sousaphones.

More than 300 members strong today, the Tiger Marching Band in 2002 received the Sudler Trophy, officially naming it the best college marching band in the country.

Maybe you can't play a lick or carry a tune in the proverbial bucket. Or perhaps you do know your way around a guitar or a keyboard and can sing "Touchdown for LSU" and "Tiger Rag" on karaoke night without closing the joint down.

Unless you're a professional musician, however, how well you play or sing really doesn't matter. What counts is that you have music in your heart and sometimes you have to turn it loose.

Worshipping God has always included music in some form. That same boisterous and musical enthusiasm you exhibit at Tiger games when the band strikes up should be a part of the joy you have in your personal worship of God.

When you consider that God loves you, he always will, and he has arranged through Jesus for you to spend eternity with him, how can that song God put in your heart not burst forth?

I like it because it plays old music.
-- Pitcher Tug McGraw on his '54 Buick

You call it music; others may call it noise;
God calls it praise.

HERO WORSHIP

Read 1 Samuel 16:1-13.

"Do not consider his appearance or his height, for . . . the Lord does not look at the things man looks at. . . . The Lord looks at the heart" (v. 7).

Ciron Black and his fellow LSU football players are heroes to a bunch of kids. For Black, though, the real hero was a kid.

Black is one of LSU's greatest offensive linemen. A four-year starter from 2006-09, he was first-team All-SEC his senior season and winner of the Jacobs Blocking Trophy as the SEC's top blocker. At 6-foot-5 and 320 pounds, Black is a big man, but the biggest part of all might be the place in his heart for a little boy named Mikey.

On Dec. 16, 2007, as he prepared for the national championship game, Black found a message on his Facebook account about an 8-year-old boy who had leukemia, who was a huge LSU fan, and who would love to get a message from a Tiger player. Black immediately replied, encouraging Mikey by reminding him that "anything is possible through Christ" and asking permission to wear his name on his wrist tape at the Jan. 7 game.

"I could hardly believe it," Mikey's mother said about the message. "When Ciron stepped into the picture, he helped us have the strength to pick up and keep going forward."

"A person like Mikey . . . teaches you not to take anything for granted and not to be so spoiled," Black said. "I was stressing

TIGERS

about finals and grades and not seeing my family, and then I hear about this little kid and he can't even be home for Christmas because he's so sick. That shook me up."

Mikey watched the championship game from his bed at St. Jude's Children's Research Hospital in Memphis. Afterwards, Black said he played the game for Mikey.

The two stayed in touch and celebrated the day Mikey went home from the hospital, his leukemia in remission.

A hero is commonly thought of as someone who performs brave and dangerous feats that save or protect someone's life. You figure that excludes you. But just ask Mikey Conger and his family if Ciron Black is a hero.

Ask your son about that when you show him how to bait a hook, or your daughter when you show up for her dance recital. Look into the eyes of those Little Leaguers you help coach.

Ask God about heroism when you're steady in your faith. For God, a hero is a person with the heart of a servant. And if a hero is a servant who acts to save other's lives, then the greatest hero of all is Jesus Christ.

God seeks heroes today, those who will proclaim the name of their hero – Jesus – proudly and boldly, no matter how others may scoff or ridicule. God knows heroes when he sees them -- by what's in their hearts.

Some people see us as heroes because of how we play, but the truth is people like yourself are the real heroes.
                                            -- Ciron Black to Mikey Conger

**God's heroes are those who remain steady
in their faith while serving others.**

ULTIMATE MAKEOVER

Read 2 Corinthians 5:11-21.

"If anyone is in Christ, he is a new creation; the old has gone, the new has come!" (v. 17)

Glen "Big Baby" Davis was angry and disappointed at himself. In response, before the 2006-07 basketball season, he made himself over, so such so that the "Big Baby" disappeared completely.

When LSU's sensational 2005-06 season ended with a loss to UCLA in the Final Four, Davis walked off the court carrying a mixture of emotions, none of them making him very happy. He had played poorly. He knew it, his teammates knew it, the whole country watching on TV knew it. So "he turned his heartache and anger into motivation." He decided he would come back to LSU for his junior season a better player.

The problem, he knew, was his body. He had allowed himself to balloon to nearly 340 pounds during the tournament. So he changed what and how he ate. He swapped his beloved cheeseburgers for some less tasty but more healthful alternatives, especially vegetables and fruit. Organic oatmeal became a morning staple. "It still tastes as nasty as ever," Davis said, but "when you are trying to accomplish what I want to, you can't eat for taste. You've got to eat for results."

Davis combined his changes in chow time with running and an aggressive weight-training program to put some definition onto his powerful body. The results were stunning; he "melted his 6-foot-9 frame to 285 pounds" and sculpted his body to "an Adonis-like torso." As incredible as it sounds, Davis started the 2006-07 season lighter than he had been at any time since the seventh grade.

The made-over made Davis first team All-SEC in 2006-07. He led the league in rebounding and was third in scoring. He left LSU as only the second player in school history (along with Shaquille O'Neal) to have 1,500 points, 900 rebounds, and 100 blocks.

Ever considered a makeover? TV shows have shown us how changes in clothes, hair, and makeup and some weight loss can radically alter the way a person looks. But these changes are only skin deep. Even with a makeover, the real you — the person inside — remains unchanged. How can you make over that part of you?

By giving your heart and soul to Jesus -- just as you give up your hair to the makeover stylist. You won't look any different; you won't dance any better; you won't suddenly start talking smarter. The change is on the inside where you are brand new because the model for all you think and feel is now Jesus. He is the one you care about pleasing.

Made over by Jesus, you realize that gaining his good opinion — not the world's — is all that really matters. And he isn't the least interested in how you look but how you act.

By the time we got to the UCLA game, I was out of shape. That showed me the results of keeping my body where it needs to be.
-- Glen Davis on his makeover

Jesus is the ultimate makeover artist; he can make you over without changing the way you look.

SMILING FACES

Read Philippians 4:4-7.

"Rejoice in the Lord always. I will say it again: Rejoice!"
(v. 4)

Reggie Robinson was smiling so big he was positively giddy. And it was the first day of spring practice 2002, for crying out loud, a time when most football players aren't exactly bubbling over with joy.

The senior wide receiver was described as "bouncing around the LSU football practice facility . . . like one of those beach balls that get batted around Tiger Stadium." A teammate wondered how Robinson could be so happy. "You don't understand," he replied. "When you have something taken away from you it's important to get it back."

What Robinson had taken away from him was football. What took it away was a pizza.

Shortly before fall practice 2001 began, Robinson reached out to hand his son some pizza. He suddenly felt "a shock-like sensation" that he knew immediately was serious. It was; he had a herniated disc and underwent surgery, which ended his season.

For a while, he wasn't sure football would ever again be a part of his life. He stayed close to the team, watching games in the stands with other players not suited up. He received an SEC championship ring.

Then in the spring, he was cleared to practice but without

contact. "Reggie is 100 percent but he will wear a redshirt in spring so we can continue to allow his neck to heal," coach Nick Saban said.

Nevertheless, the injury was on Robinson's mind, especially when he took a tumble in practice after catching a pass. "There's a little soreness," he said. "Not from the surgery, but from having a helmet back on my head."

Then he smiled. "Before I would just go to practice," he said. "Now I'm happy to go." He went on to play in all but one of LSU's games in 2002, catching seven passes for 119 yards.

What does your smile say about you? What makes you smile in the first place? Your dad's corny jokes? Don Knotts as Barney Fife? Your children or grandchildren? Your pal's bad imitations? Do you hoard your smile, or do you give it away easily even when you've had some tough times?

When you smile, the ones who love you and whom you love can't help but return the favor -- and the joy. It's like turning on a bright light in a world threatened by darkness. Besides, you have good reason to walk around all the time with a smile on your face not because of something you have done but rather because of one basic, unswerving truth: God loves you. As a result of his great love for you, God acted through Jesus to give you free and eternal salvation. That should certainly make you smile.

The bat is gone but the smile remains.
-- Baseball Hall of Famer Willie Stargell

It so overused it's become a cliché, but it's true nevertheless: Smile! God loves you.

DAY 35

MOVING ON

Read Colossians 3:5-17.

"You have taken off your old self with its practices and have put on the new self" (vv. 9-10).

Trains, boats, and planes – not to mention campers, motorcycles, and pickup trucks. Whatever it takes, Tiger fans will use it to get to an LSU football game.

For the Tulane game in New Orleans in 1919, LSU's cadets couldn't afford the round-trip rail fare of $2.40, so about 75 of them climbed aboard a freight train as it passed through Baton Rouge about 1 a.m. the day of the game. A brakeman discovered the moochers and threatened to call the police when the train arrived in New Orleans. Some smooth talkers in the group, however, convinced the railroad employee – obviously an LSU fan -- that "any mode of travel was proper if the objective was a football game between their school and its biggest rival."

The cheeky cadets even managed to rip off a meal, making a breakfast of some sugar cane that was aboard the freight. They also procured a ride back home as the brakeman offered to let them hop the Sunday freight. They didn't need his generosity, however. The Tigers pulled off a shocking 27-6 upset of Tulane behind two touchdowns from fullback Joe Bernstein, who ran behind star lineman Tom Dutton. The cadets had placed a bet on the game and rode home in style on a passenger train.

The Tigers were likewise big underdogs in 1922, but that didn't

TIGERS

keep fans from getting to the game any way they could. A traffic survey in Baton Rouge counted 2,280 automobiles, nine motorcycles, 32 horseback riders, 21 buggies, 50 horse-drawn vehicles, two bicycles, one tractor, and 30 weary folks on foot making their way into town.

Behind two touchdowns from Roland Kizer and one each from Reggie McFarland and Gus Jackson, LSU again pulled the upset, 25-14. Those traveling fans went home happy.

We have always been a nation on the move. Pioneers seeking a better life spread out across unfamiliar territory and in the process conquered the American wilderness. That wanderlust seems part of our national character now, and you probably inherited it. A new job, a new home, better schools for the kids -- you'll load up a U-Haul truck or the back of a pickup and head out to a new place for any number of reasons. You leave the old behind and embrace the new, knowing you can never turn back -- and not wanting to.

An encounter with Jesus Christ has a similar effect on a person's life. You leave behind the old ways; new habits beckon. You move on to a different, new, and even unfamiliar you with no desire to ever again be what you were before.

Jesus never gives you the option of turning back, so with your eyes and your heart fixed on the road ahead, you move on, heading resolutely toward bigger, better, and more glorious days.

If you stand still, there's only one way to go, and that's backwards.
-- Soccer legend Peter Shilton

**An encounter with Jesus Christ sets a life
on a journey with glory as its final destination.**

LESSON LEARNED

Read Matthew 11:20-30.

"Take my yoke upon you and learn from me" (v. 29).

O ne of football's tried-and-true strategies is to call a time out to "ice" the kicker when he is about to attempt a game-winning field goal in the closing seconds. Once, however, an LSU kicker called the time out himself -- because he had learned a lesson.

In 1964, the Bayou Bengals went 7-2-1 and earned a Sugar Bowl bid, thanks in no small part to the heroics of junior flanker Doug Moreau. The Tigers got inside their opponents' ten yard line 21 times that season but scored only five touchdowns. This forced LSU frequently "to turn to a weapon that was an afterthought in those days: the field goal." Moreau kicked thirteen field goals during the regular season, an NCAA record.

Moreau had never kicked a field goal until he arrived at LSU. He was a self-taught kicker, thanks to a telephone line that stretched across his yard at home. It was the perfect enticement for a kid looking to kick a football.

Moreau was indispensable in 1964. He won the opener over Texas A&M 9-6 with a 34-yard field goal. A week later, his late kick edged Rice 3-0. His kick notched a 3-3 tie with Tennessee. He caught the two-point conversion that whipped Ole Miss late 11-10 and snared both touchdown passes in a 14-10 win over Mississippi State.

Thus, when crunch time came in the Sugar Bowl against

TIGERS

favored Syracue, the Tigers turned to Moreau. With 3:48 to play, the score was tied at 10 as LSU lined up for a 28-yard kick. The Orangemen were out of time outs, but LSU called one. "I needed it," Moreau said.

It seems he had missed a kick against Mississippi State because he had been winded from running pass routes. "I remembered that and used this [time out] to catch my breath," Moreau said.

He learned a lesson, the kick was good, and LSU won 13-10.

Learning about anything in life requires a combination of education and experience. Education is the accumulation of facts that we call knowledge; experience is the acquisition of wisdom and discernment, which add purpose and understanding to our knowledge.

The most difficult way to learn is trial and error: dive in blindly and mess up. The best way to learn is through example coupled with a set of instructions: Someone has gone ahead of you and has written down all the information you need to follow.

In teaching us the way to live godly lives, God chose the latter method. He set down in his book the habits, actions, and attitudes that make for a way of life in accordance with his wishes. He also sent us Jesus to explain and to illustrate.

God teaches us not just how to exist but how to live. We just need to be attentive students.

The Lord taught me to love everybody, but the last ones I learned to love were the sportswriters.
> *– LSU tailback and baseball legend Alvin Dark*

To learn from Jesus is to learn what life is all about and how God means for us to live it.

IN THE BAD TIMES

Read Philippians 1:3-14.

"What has happened to me has really served to advance the gospel. . . . Because of my chains, most of the brothers in the Lord have been encouraged to speak the word of God more courageously and fearlessly" (vv. 12, 14).

Brandon Bass knew the bad times that squelched his dreams, so he helped some kids enjoy some good times.

Bass spent only two years in Baton Rouge before he turned pro after the 2005 season, but he had quite a career as a Tiger. He started every game both seasons and was the SEC Freshman of the Year in 2004. In 2005, he was the SEC Player of the Year, the first Tiger to win the award since Shaquille O'Neal in 1992. He was also the league's scholar-athlete of the year and an honorable mention All-America. In 2005, he led the Tigers to a 20-10 season, the Western Division championship, and the NCAA Tournament. He averaged 15.1 points and 8.3 rebounds per game as a Tiger. He was drafted in the second round and became a millionaire.

But Bass knew bad times long before the good times came. When he was ten, his 32-year-old mother died of a heart attack right in front of him. He moved with his younger brother and sister into their father's house, but the arrangement didn't work out. Soon, they moved again to live with an aunt.

During this troublesome time, Bass didn't play any basketball, his skills lying dormant. "All I did was ride my bike all day during the summer," he recalled. When he was 13, he began playing the game again, though he never attended a basketball camp. "Couldn't afford it," he said matter-of-factly. He also remembered that he "didn't have any inspiration, just bad influences."

Bass never forgot those bad times, and he has used some of his wealth to stage camps for underprivileged kids in Louisiana. "God has just blessed me in so many ways," he said. "I've had to go through a lot. Now I just want to give something back."

Loved ones die. You're downsized. Your biopsy looks cancerous. Your spouse could be having an affair. Hard, tragic times are as much a part of life as breath.

This applies to Christians too. Christianity is not the equivalent of a Get-out-of-Jail-Free card, granting us a lifelong exemption from either the least or the worst pain the world has to offer. While Jesus promises us he will be there to lead us through the valleys, he never promises that we will not enter them.

The question thus becomes how you handle the bad times. You can buckle to your knees in despair and cry, "Why me?" Or you can hit your knees in prayer and ask, "What do I do with this?"

Setbacks and tragedies are opportunities to reveal and to develop true character and abiding faith. Your faithfulness -- not your skipping merrily along through life without pain -- is what reveals the depth of your love for God.

If I said, "God, why me?" about the bad things, then I should have said, "God, why me?" about the good things that happened in my life.
— Arthur Ashe

Faithfulness to God requires faith even in
-- especially in -- the bad times.

DAY 38

FRUIT TREES

Read Matthew 7:15-20.

"By their fruit you will recognize them" (v. 20).

Fruit -- specifically oranges -- was the order of the night on Dec. 5, 1970, when the Tigers blasted Ole Miss 61-17.

As time wound down in the one-sided win, LSU students pelted the field with hundreds of oranges. There was a method to their orange-flavored madness, however. The win -- the biggest over Ole Miss since a 52-7 spanking in 1917 -- locked up both the SEC championship and an Orange Bowl bid for the Tigers.

Only after the public address announcer warned the "fantastically fired-up LSU fans" to stop tossing oranges or their beloved Tigers would be penalized did the barrage come to a temporary halt. After yet another Bayou Bengal score, though, the oranges took flight again, prompting one frustrated Ole Miss player to pick up an orange and toss it back toward the riotous LSU stands.

The game was expected to be a close one, even with legendary Ole Miss quarterback Archie Manning hobbled by an injury. The Tigers came in 8-2; Ole Miss entered the game at 7-2 with a Gator Bowl bid locked up.

The Rebs scored the game's first touchdown, but the rest of the night belonged to the Tigers. They led 23-10 at halftime and 33-17 after three quarters before pouring it on with a 28-0 blitz in the final period. All-American Tommy Casanova had two punt returns for touchdowns, becoming the first SEC player in history and the third in college football history to accomplish the feat. Craig Burns also scampered 61 yards with a punt for a third touchdown, tying the NCAA record.

As the oranges rained down, LSU Coach Charles McClendon called the romp "the most important victory of my life." The president of the Orange Bowl declared LSU's win to be "one of the most tremendous football games I have ever seen."

Strawberry shortcake. Apple pie. Ice-cold watermelon. Banana pudding. Straight up, congealed, or served with whipped cream or ice cream, fresh fruit -- including oranges -- is hard to beat. We even use it symbolically to represent the good things in our lives: A promotion or a raise is the fruit of our good work.

Fruity metaphors and images conjure up thoughts of something sweet and satisfying. Little in life, however, is as rancid as fruit gone bad. That dual image of fruit at its best and its worst is what Jesus had in mind when he spoke of knowing both false prophets and faithful followers by their fruit.

Our lives as disciples of Jesus should yield not just material fruits but spiritual fruits also. Our spiritual fruits are what we leave in our wake: heartbreak, tears, anger, bitterness, and dissension; or peace, love, joy, generosity, and gentleness.

Good or bad – delicious or rotten -- these are the fruits by which we shall be known by those around us – and by God.

[The LSU win] assures the Orange Bowl the best bowl game ever, not only of those bowls this New Year's but ever.
-- Orange Bowl President W. Keith Phillips Jr. after the 61-17 win

God knows you by your spiritual fruits,
not the material ones the world fancies so.

HOME IMPROVEMENT

Read Ephesians 4:7-16.

"The body of Christ may be built up until we all reach unity in the faith and in the knowledge of the Son of God and become mature, attaining to the whole measure of the fullness of Christ" (vv. 12b, 13).

He is one of the greatest players in the history of both collegiate and professional basketball, yet by his own admission, the first time he picked a ball up, he was "terrible."

Bob Pettit was the first LSU athlete to have his number retired. He is a member of both the LSU and the pro basketball halls of fame. A street in Baton Rouge is named for him. He is credited with creating the power forward position as it is played today and was the first Most Valuable Player in NBA history. At LSU from 1952-55, he averaged 27.8 points per game and was three times All-SEC and twice All-America.

Pettit was so bad when he started out, however, that he was cut from the varsity team in both his freshman and sophomore years of high school -- and he didn't disagree with the coach's decision. "I had never played basketball, was thin, didn't have any talent, and was really uncoordinated," Pettit said of himself. "In short, I was terrible."

He was on the roster for the junior or "B" team as a high-school freshman. but he occupied the last spot on the team. Once when the team bus broke down before a game, he was left behind

TIGERS

because there wasn't enough room in cars for everyone.

So how did he go from terrible to terrific? He worked at it. After he was cut a second time, he practiced every evening after school for hours, ate supper, and then practiced some more. And he kept working at it over the years, once declaring that his being terrible was the best thing that ever happened to him because it pushed him to improve.

Just as Bob Pettit did, you try to improve at whatever you tackle. You attend training sessions and seminars to do your job better. You take golf or tennis lessons and practice to get better. You play that new video game until you master it. To get better at anything requires a dedication involving practice, training, study, and preparation.

Your faith life is no different. Jesus calls us to improve ourselves spiritually by becoming more mature in our faith. We can always know more about God's word, discover more ways to serve God, deepen our prayer life and our trust in God, and do a better job of being Jesus to other people through simple acts of kindness and caring. In other words, we can always become more like Jesus.

One day we will all stand before God as finished products. We certainly want to present him a mature dwelling, a spiritual mansion, not a hovel.

If things come naturally, you might not bother to work at improving them and you can fall short of your potential.
*   -- Bob Pettit*

Spiritual improvement means a constant effort
to become more like Jesus in our day-to-day lives.

NO PLACE LIKE HOME

Read Joshua 24:14-27.

*"Choose for yourselves this day whom you will serve. . . .
But as for me and my household, we will serve the Lord"
(v. 15).*

It's been called one of the most intimidating, dreaded road sites in all of college football. Its nickname, "Death Valley," is totally appropriate because it's where teams' hopes go to die. It's LSU's Tiger Stadium.

In the 1920s, a completely new LSU campus was constructed three miles south of Baton Rouge on two plantations. Part of that construction was a new football stadium. Expectations were that the stadium would be ready for the Tulane game on Thanksgiving Day 1924. Some of it was. The concrete stands weren't completed, so temporary bleachers were set up, and the unfinished section of the stadium was roped off.

Another major problem with the new facility was how to get folks to it. Adequate roads for cars between Baton Rouge and the new campus simply didn't exist. The railroad tracks did pass close to the stadium, so a shuttle train was set up to run between the city and the stadium to transport the bulk of the crowd.

The new facility didn't have any dressing rooms. Tulane improvised by dressing on the train while the LSU team suited up in its old quarters downtown and rode taxis to a completed building near the stadium. They walked the rest of the way.

TIGERS

A crowd of about 18,500 showed up for that first game. Numerous renovations and improvements have enlarged the seating capacity to more than 92,000 today, making Tiger Stadium the seventh-largest on-campus facility in the country.

A stadium tradition began in 1931 with a night game against Spring Hill. This has only made what was already a formidable home-field advantage even more daunting. LSU has won better than seven out of every ten games played in Tiger Stadium.

You enter your home to find love, security, and joy. It's the place where your heart feels warmest, your laughter comes easiest, and your life is its richest. It is the center of and the reason for everything you do and everything you are.

How can a home be such a place?

If it is a home where grace is spoken before every meal, it is such a place. If it is a home where the Bible is read, studied, and discussed by the whole family gathered together, it is such a place. If it is a home that serves as a jumping-off point for the whole family to go to church, not just on Sunday morning and not just occasionally, but regularly, it is such a place. If it is a home where the name of God is spoken with reverence and awe and not with disrespect and indifference, it is such a place.

In other words, a house becomes a true home when God is part of the family.

There are very few stadiums in America worth a touchdown, but the Bayou Bengals certainly have that advantage in Tiger Stadium.
-- ESPN reporter Adrian Karsten

**A home is full when all the family members –
including God -- are present.**

TRUSTWORTHY

Read Psalm 25.

"To you, O lord, I lift up my soul. In you I trust, O my God" (vv. 1-2).

Because the opposing coach trusted LSU's head man, Gaynell Tinsley, the Tigers got a Sugar Bowl bid.

When Ken Konz, one of LSU's all-time great defensive backs, ran a Tulane punt back 92 yards for a touchdown in the opening minutes of the 1949 game, Sugar Bowl officials started fretting. They were in New Orleans to invite the Green Wave to the bowl game in the wake of their expected victory. After LSU's 21-0 win, they were really in a mess.

They couldn't just invite LSU; an SEC rule required a winning percentage the Tigers didn't have. So a whole series of intense negotiations took place on Sunday, Nov. 27. LSU's athletic director, T.P. Heard, burned up the phone lines and got the other conference athletic directors to agree to waive the rule if the Tigers got a Sugar Bowl invitation.

But another problem remained. Oklahoma was already in the bowl game, and the Sooner head coach, Bud Wilkinson, was not at all enthusiastic about playing LSU. His team had won everything in sight, but Tulane had been a powerful team too, so Wilkinson had seen what the Tigers were capable of. Oklahoma had nothing to gain and much to lose by playing LSU.

So the negotiations continued on into the night. A newspaper

TIGERS

reported that "the group sitting in Coach Tinsley's office . . . saw their hopes go up and down like an elevator." Finally, though, a break came and LSU was in.

That "break" was a verbal agreement between LSU and Oklahoma. Tinsley agreed not to recruit in the state of Oklahoma, and because the Sooner coach knew Tinsley could be trusted, he agreed to the bowl game. Trust won the day for LSU.

The benefits and boons our modern age has given us have come at a price. One of those costs is the erosion of our trusting nature. Once upon a time in America we trusted until we saw a reason not to. Now, wariness is our first response to most situations.

It's not just outlandish claims on TV that have rendered us a nation of skeptics. We've come to accept hucksters as relatively harmless scam artists who are part of living in a capitalistic society.

No, the serious damage to our inherent sense of trust has been done in our personal relationships. With much pain, we have learned the truth: Many people just flat can't be trusted.

Ant then there's God, whom we can trust absolutely. He will not let us down; he is incapable of lying to us; he always delivers on his promises; he is always there when we need him.

In God we can trust. It sounds like a motto we might find on a coin, but it's a statement of absolute truth.

We've made an agreement and we'll live up to it.
-- Gaynell Tinsley on his promise to Bud Wilkinson

We look for the scam before surrendering our trust, but we can trust God without hesitation.

DAY 42

GOOD SPORTS

Read Titus 2:1-8.

"Show integrity, seriousness and soundness of speech that cannot be condemned, so that those who oppose you may be ashamed because they have nothing bad to say about us" (vv. 7b, 8).

Winning regionals is certainly nothing exceptional for the LSU baseball team, so claiming another one in June 2003 wasn't particularly remarkable. What happened after the final game ended, however, was.

Jon Zeringue's walk-off home run in the 11th inning at Alex Box Stadium ended the season for UNC-Wilmington and propelled the Tigers on to a super regional with a thrilling 9-8 win. Throughout the tournament, the LSU fans had bonded with the Seahawks, packing the stadium to cheer for them against archrival Tulane in the opening round and then cheering for them again the next day when UNCW eliminated Tulane in extra innings. Many fans mixed their LSU gear with UNCW shirts.

So as the Seahawk players gathered by their dugout in disappointment, an LSU employee walked over and said, "Guys, they'd like you to take a lap." "Who?" a player asked. "The fans."

The players then looked along the baselines in shock. Tiger fans were crowding along the fence, extending their arms to the opposing players. Others were on their feet applauding and chanting "Seahawks!"

TIGERS

The victory lap is an LSU baseball tradition. The players circle the stands, giving high-fives to the fans lining the grandstand and leaning over the outfield wall. It had never been offered to an opponent until that day.

So the amazed and smiling Seahawks took their victory lap on this day when the fans took some of the sting out of a defeat with a wonderful act of sportsmanship.

One of life's paradoxes is that many who would never consider cheating on the tennis court or the racquetball court to gain an advantage think nothing of doing so in other areas of their life. In other words, the good sportsmanship they practice on the golf course or even on the Monopoly board doesn't carry over.

They play with the truth, cut corners, abuse others verbally, run roughshod over the weaker, and generally cheat whenever they can to gain an advantage on the job or in their personal relationships.

But good sportsmanship is a way of living, not just of playing. Shouldn't you accept defeat without complaint (You don't have to like it.); win gracefully without gloating; treat your competition with fairness, courtesy, generosity, and respect? That's the way one team treats another in the name of sportsmanship. That's the way one person treats another in the name of Jesus.

I've never seen anything like this.
-- A reporter on the UNCW victory lap

Sportsmanship -- treating others with courtesy, fairness, and respect -- is a way of living, not just a way of playing.

DAY 43

FOOD FOR THOUGHT

Read Genesis 9:1-7.

"Everything that lives and moves will be food for you. Just as I gave you the green plants, I now give you everything" (v. 3).

The proposed solution to a shortage of food for Mike the Tiger drew such ire from the students that they kidnapped and encaged the top student leaders and paraded them around campus.

World War II affected even Mike I. His typical daily diet was ten pounds of steak donated by a local company. In 1943, though, because of meat rationing, neither the local company nor LSU officials could procure enough steak for Mike. His choice meat was replaced by what was called "scrap beef." Before long, though, even scraps were in short supply. The proud symbol of LSU athletics was reduced to eating horse meat and cereal.

A solution seemed to present itself when arrangements were made to move Mike to Audubon Zoo in New Orleans for the duration of the war. The facility had several thousand pounds of meat in cold storage. The student body, however, was not at all receptive to the notion of sending Mike into the lair of Tulane, their greatest football rival at the time.

The students were so riled up about the whole deal that on the proposed day of Mike's departure, some protestors kidnapped the student body president and vice president, locked them in Mike's traveling cage, and pushed them around campus. Alarmed, the

TIGERS

administration decided to allow students to vote on the issue.

In the four-day interval, the official reason for sending Mike to New Orleans changed. Now it wasn't merely a matter of food -- which Mike may well have considered reason enough -- but the problem of an heir. Mike was getting old and time was growing short. Given this reason, the students relented.

Belly up to the buffet, boys and girls, for barbecue, sirloin steak, grilled chicken, and fried catfish with hush puppies and cheese grits. Rachael Ray's a household name; hamburger joints, pizza parlors, and taco stands lurk on every corner; and we have a TV channel devoted exclusively to food. We love our chow and generally don't have the problem Mike had in getting it.

Food is one of God's really good ideas, but consider the complex divine plan that begins with a seed and ends with French fries. The creator of all life devised a system in which living things are sustained and nourished physically through the sacrifice of other living things in a way similar to what Christ underwent to save us spiritually. Whether it's fast food or home-cooked, everything we eat is a gift from God secured through a divine plan in which some plants and animals have given up their lives.

Pausing to give thanks before we dive in seems the least we can do.

I am on as close terms with Mike as possible, and he's soon going to curl up and die.
-- LSU coach William G. Higginbotham on the need to move Mike

**God created a system that nourishes us
through the sacrifice of other living things;
that's worth a thank-you.**

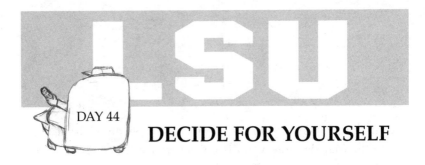

DECIDE FOR YOURSELF

Read John 6:60-69.

"The words I have spoken to you are spirit and they are life. Yet there are some of you who do not believe" (vv. 63b-64a).

The only two jobs Charles McClendon ever wanted came open the same day and were both offered to him. He decided for one first but ultimately decided for the other.

After coaching the 1961 Tigers to a 10-1 record that included the SEC championship and an Orange-Bowl win over Colorado, Paul Dietzel asked the Board of Supervisors to release him from his contract so he could become the head coach at Army. Some board members thought he should stay and coach for the four years still on his contract, but after some heated debate, the board granted Dietzel's request. Athletic Director Jim Corbett immediately announced LSU would not take applications for the job but would select the coaches it wished to consider and contact them.

That same day, McClendon, one of Dietzel's assistants, had been offered the head coaching job at Kentucky, his alma mater. "I told them to give me a day to think it over," McClendon said. He decided to take it because it was one of his dream jobs.

Before he gave Kentucky an answer, though, McClendon wanted to talk to Corbett. He found him at the home of LSU President Dr. John Hunter and told them, "Fellows, I wanted you to know, I've decided to go to Kentucky."

TIGERS

That spurred Corbett into a flurry of phone calls to board members. "It was kind of funny, " McClendon recalled. "We were talking in a bedroom, and they maneuvered me behind the bed and wouldn't let me get to a phone where I could call Kentucky."

When Corbett finished his phone calls, he told McClendon the LSU job was his for the taking. McClendon made another decision, calling Kentucky and telling them he was going to stay at LSU

As with Charles McClendon, the decisions you have made along the way have shaped your life at every pivotal moment. Some decisions you made suddenly and carelessly; some you made carefully and deliberately; some were forced upon you. You may have learned that some of those spur-of-the-moment decisions have turned out better than your carefully considered ones.

Of all your life's decisions, however, none is more important than one you cannot ignore: What have you done with Jesus? Even in his time, people chose to follow Jesus or to reject him, and nothing has changed; the decision must still be made and nobody can make it for you. Ignoring Jesus won't work either; that is, in fact, a decision, and neither he nor the consequences of your decision will go away.

Considered or spontaneous – how you arrive at a decision for Jesus doesn't matter; all that matters is that you get there.

The only two jobs I had wanted, LSU and my alma mater, both came open and were offered to me the same day. It was unreal.
-- Charles McClendon

A decision for Jesus may be spontaneous or considered; what counts is that you make it.

THE PIONEER SPIRIT

Read Luke 5:1-11.

"So they pulled their boats up on shore, left everything and followed him" (v. 11).

The Lady Tigers' media guide declares that 1975-76 was the first season of women's basketball. The true pioneers, however, first took the court some 66 years before.

The LSU basketball program was born on Jan. 30, 1909, "in a poorly lighted hall of an academy located in Covington" before what was basically a mere handful of spectators. The men's team had a 5-2 record under head coach E.R. Wingard that initial season. The captain was W.J. "Red" Phillips. That initial game was a 35-20 win over Dixon Academy.

The win apparently was an upset. As *The New Advocate* in Baton Rouge reported, "This victory was quite a surprise to admirers of the local team, who little expected such glad tidings." The paper said the LSU boys were underdogs because the game was played indoors under the lights and the locals had practiced outdoors the whole time. One player reported "they were royally entertained by their hosts and were delighted" with the win.

That victory set the team on the way to a four-game win streak that included an 18-12 victory over Mississippi State in the first-ever home game. The streak came to a screeching halt, however, with a double dip against the New Orleans YMCA.

The guys weren't the only pioneers in 1909 as "that same season,

TIGERS

the LSU coeds also went in for basketball." The 1909 *Gumbo*, the school yearbook, gave scant coverage to the women's team, however, noting simply that they were "only defeated once."

Those trailblazers for LSU women's basketball were Annie Boyd, for whom a dormitory is named, Lucille McKowen, Essie Gauthreaux, Nora Doughtery, Winnie Maine, Lula Norwood, and Ida Howell.

Going to a place in your life you've never been before -- such as collegiate basketball -- requires a willingness to take risks and face uncertainty head-on. You may have never helped start a new sports program at a major college, but you've had your moments when your latent pioneer spirit manifested itself. That time you changed careers, ran a marathon, volunteered at a homeless shelter, learned Spanish, or went back to school.

While attempting new things invariably begets apprehension, the truth is that when life becomes too comfortable and too familiar, it gets boring. The same is true of God, who is downright dangerous because he calls us to be anything but comfortable as we serve him. He summons us to continuously blaze new trails in our faith life, to follow him no matter what. Stepping out on faith is risky all right, but the reward is a life of accomplishment, adventure, and joy that cannot be equaled anywhere else.

Life is an adventure. I wouldn't want to know what's going to happen next.

-- *Bobby Bowden*

**Unsafe and downright dangerous, God calls us
out of the place where we are comfortable
to a life of adventure and trailblazing in his name.**

CALLING IT QUITS

Read Numbers 13:25-14:4.

"The men who had gone up with him said, 'We can't attack those people; they are stronger than we are'" (v. 13:31).

Expecting sympathy when he told his father he was quitting football at LSU, Jerry Stovall didn't get any. So he changed his mind and changed LSU football history.

When Stovall arrived on campus in 1958, he didn't look like much. He was the last prospect Coach Paul Dietzel signed in a class of 52 players, and Stovall admitted that with his spectacles and his quiet disposition he "was the runt of the litter." His high-school coach said, "No one in their right mind would've figured him to be an All-American," which Stovall became -- twice.

But all that acclaim and a nine-year, Pro-Bowl professional career lay ahead of him when, as a freshman, Stovall found himself just another face in a crowd that included some very good football players. It didn't take long for Stovall to discover "there were lots of bigger, faster, stronger players than me."

He became discouraged and called his father to tell him he wanted to come home. The senior Stovall's reply was both blunt and practical. He told his son to come on home; he would find him a job. That caused the younger Stoval to pause. After all, his father was a salesman who climbed out of bed every morning at five to get started on his rounds.

TIGERS

"There wasn't a lot of sympathy there," Stovall said of his dad. After all, Stovall senior was working from dawn to dusk to keep food on the table and "must have been irked listening to his boy complain about how difficult it had become to play a game."

Jerry took a minute to think about the kind of job his dad would secure for him and he heard the exasperation in his father's voice. Then he "told Dad that maybe I'd give football a chance for just a little longer."

He never again considered quitting.

Remember that time you quit a high-school sports team? Bailed out of a relationship? Walked away from that job with the goals unachieved? Sometimes quitting is the most sensible way to minimize your losses, so you may well at times in your life give up on something or someone.

In your relationship with God, however, you should remember the people of Israel, who quit when the Promised Land was theirs for the taking. They forgot one fact of life you never should: God never gives up on you.

That means you should never, ever give up on God. No matter how tired or discouraged you get, no matter that it seems your prayers aren't getting through to God, no matter what – quitting on God is not an option. He is preparing a blessing for you, and in his time, he will bring it to fruition -- if you don't quit on him.

Once you learn to quit, it becomes a habit.

– Vince Lombardi

Whatever else you give up on in your life, don't give up on God; he will never ever give up on you.

EXCUSES, EXCUSES

Read Luke 9:57-62.

"Another said, 'I will follow you, Lord; but first let me go back and say good-by to my family'" (v. 61).

The LSU football players were spending too much time on their classwork. That was the rather novel excuse once given for a loss; there was no excuse -- or explanation -- however, for another loss that occurred that season.

Football was still taking shape at the turn of the twentieth century and was still subject to the vagaries of society and technology. For instance, both the 1897 and the 1898 seasons were virtually lost to a pair of yellow fever epidemics that both years delayed the start of school. Anyone wishing to enter or leave Baton Rouge had to obtain a permit, and even the mail was fumigated. LSU managed only two games for the 1897 season -- versus the Montgomery Athletic Club and a touring team from Cincinnati -- and played only a single game against Tulane in 1898.

By 1900 football in Baton Rouge was back in full swing, though not necessarily successfully. The team opened the season by smashing Millsaps College 70-0. Then came a 29-0 walloping at the hands of Tulane. While staunch LSU fans of the day may well have argued that there was no excuse for losing to Tulane, two excuses nevertheless emerged. The first was "overconfidence" since LSU "had been so occasioned to running through Tulane's teams in the past without any special effort." A second excuse as claimed in the *Daily Advocate*, though, was one not likely to be heard today. The editor declared that the football players "had been doing such splendid classwork that they have not had the opportunity to devote the necessary time to field practice."

Be that as it may, no excuse could be found for what happened when LSU went to Jackson, Miss., for a return game with Millsaps, victim of the 70-0 smashing less than three weeks before. Millsaps won 6-5.

Has some of your most creative thinking involved excuses for not going in to work? Have you discovered that an unintended benefit of computers is that you can always blame them for the destruction of all your hard work? Don't you manage to stammer or stutter some justification when a state trooper pulls you over? We're usually pretty good at making excuses to cover our failures or to get out of something we don't particularly want to do.

That holds true for our faith life also. The Bible is too hard to understand so I won't read it; the weather's too pretty to be shut up in church; praying in public is embarrassing and I'm not very good at it anyway. The plain truth is, though, that whatever excuses we make for not following Jesus wholeheartedly are not good enough.

Jesus made no excuses to avoid dying for us; we should offer none to avoid living for him.

There are a thousand reasons for failure but not a single excuse.
-- Former NFL player Mike Reid

Try though we might, no excuses can justify
our failure to follow Jesus wholeheartedly.

JUST PERFECT

Read Matthew 5:43-48.

"Be perfect, therefore, as your heavenly Father is perfect"
(v. 48).

If you study this game carefully, you'll find that LSU has played a perfect game." They had to.

The speaker was a sportswriter in the press box after the 1966 Cotton Bowl. Thanks largely to the persuasive powers of athletic director Jim Corbett, the Tigers received an invitation to the Dallas bowl game. "Many football fans around the land thought both LSU and the Cotton Bowl had blown a fuse."

The Tigers were only 7-3 and had been beaten badly twice. Their opponent was Arkansas, which had won 22 straight games and had led the nation in scoring defense two years running. They had won the national championship in 1964 and had their sights on another one with the expected win over LSU in Dallas.

"The Tigers were hopelessly outmatched in personnel," but Coach Charles McClendon had them superbly prepared to pull off one of the greatest upsets in LSU football history.

The game didn't start out very promising as the Razorbacks marched 87 yards on their first possession to lead 7-0. But the Tigers returned the favor and shook everyone up by marching 80 yards against that supposedly impregnable Arkansas defense. Senior Joe Labruzzo followed the blocking of Dave McCormick and Don Ellen on four straight cracks into the line that capped

TIGERS

the drive. Doug Moreau's extra point tied the game.

Tiger center Bill Bass recovered a Razorback fumble on the 34, and Labruzzo, McCormick, and Ellen did it again with basic power plays five straight times from the 19. LSU led 14-7 at halftime, and the lead held up, the big play a late interception by cornerback Jerry Joseph. The Tigers had played a "perfect" game.

Nobody's really perfect; we all make mistakes every day. We botch our personal relationships; at work we seek competence, not perfection. To insist upon personal or professional perfection in our lives is to establish an impossibly high standard that eventually destroys us physically, emotionally, and mentally.

Yet that is exactly the standard God sets for us. Our love is to be perfect, never ceasing, never failing, never qualified – just the way God loves us. And Jesus didn't limit his command to only preachers and goody-two-shoes types. All of his disciples are to be perfect as they navigate their way through the world's ambiguous definition and understanding of love.

But that's impossible! Well, not necessarily if to love perfectly is to serve God wholeheartedly and to follow Jesus with single-minded devotion. Anyhow, in his perfect love for us, God makes allowance for our imperfect love and the consequences of it in the perfection of Jesus.

We didn't make a mistake. Some people didn't think we could play this kind of football.
--Coach Charles McClendon after the 1966 Cotton Bowl

In his perfect love for us, God provides a way
for us to escape the consequences
of our imperfect love for him: Jesus.

DAY 49

THE SIMPLE LIFE

Read 1 John 1:5-10.

"If we confess our sins, he is faithful and just and will forgive us our sins and purify us from all unrighteousness" (v. 9).

Y ou have ten guys and only one basketball. If I have the ball, who can beat me?"

That was the simple, winning formula espoused by the first basketball All-America in LSU history.

Malcolm "Sparky" Wade came to Baton Rouge in 1931 "with a dollar in his pocket and some sandwiches wrapped in an old bandana." He also arrived with "an inordinate desire to excel" that was perhaps engendered by his size: He was only 5'6" tall.

Before there was the "Pistol," there was "Sparky." His play on the court was driven by his belief that "basketball is the silliest game in the world" because the player controlling the ball would win the game. Thus, he developed himself into the player who controlled the ball. He was "a super showman," a "bantam preview of the later [Pete] Maravich" who "could shoot, pass, and literally do anything with a basketball, including dance on it." Wade was such a spectacular ball handler that "he was confident he could go one-on-one with anybody and maintain possession of the ball until he was ready to let it go." Thus, his simple formula.

In 1935, Wade's senior season, in an age before the NCAA tournament, the Tigers played Pittsburgh in the American Legion

TIGERS

Bowl in Atlantic City for what was the "mythical" national championship. The Panthers determined that they would stop Wade, so they double- and triple-teamed him the entire game. Wade couldn't score, but he could still control the ball. That was quite enough. He spent the night hitting Nathan "Buddy" Blair and Lloyd Lindsey with perfect passes, and LSU won 41-37.

Perhaps the simple life in America was doomed by the arrival of the programmable VCR. Since then, we've been on an inevitably downward spiral into ever more complicated lives. Even windshield wipers have multiple settings now, and it takes a graduate degree to figure out clothes dryers.

But we might do well in our own lives to mimic the simple formula Sparky Wade used to play basketball. That is, we should approach our lives with the keen awareness that success requires simplicity. We should stick to the basics: Revere God, love our families, honor our country, do our best.

Theologians may make what God did in Jesus as complicated as quantum mechanics and the infield fly rule, but God kept it simple for us: believe, trust, and obey. Believe in Jesus as the Son of God, trust that through him God makes possible our deliverance from our sins into Heaven, and obey God in the way he wants us to live. It's simple, but it's the true winning formula, the way to win for all eternity.

I think God made it simple. Just accept Him and believe.
-- Bobby Bowden

Life continues to get ever more complicated,
but God made it simple for us
when he showed up as Jesus.

DAY 50

EARTHMOVERS

Read Psalm 100.

"Shout for joy to the Lord, all the earth!" (v. 1)

It is the stuff of legend, only in LSU's case, it's true. One night in Baton Rouge, the LSU crowd did indeed make the earth move.

On Oct. 8, 1988, the Tigers hosted Auburn in a key SEC showdown. Auburn led 6-0 with only 1:47 left to play when Tommy Hodson threw a fourth-down touchdown pass to tailback Eddie Fuller. The spontaneous eruption of joy from the 80,000 or so fans in Tiger Stadium registered as an earthquake on the seismograph in the LSU Geology Department.

It's the sort of story that achieves mythic proportions, so it tends to become disregarded as mere folklore. Even Fuller admits, "Initially, I didn't believe it." But in the early 1990s he was going through the Ripley's Believe It or Not Museum in Niagara Falls, "and I looked up and there it was." Hodson said he recalled seeing a photo of the seismograph reading in the student newspaper.

While the fans were surprised to learn their reaction had registered on a seismograph, LSU's geologists were downright stunned. "It was a total surprise," said Riley Milner, a research associate.

One matter for debate ever since is whether it was the shout or the jumping up and down that registered on the seismograph. LSU geology professors generally agree it was the jumping up and down that probably produced a low-frequency sound wave that traveled through the upper layers of the earth.

TIGERS

The force of the game itself should have registered on seismographs all night. Both Hodson and Fuller agreed it was the most physical game they had ever played. The Tiger defense held fourth-ranked Auburn to only two field goals. Auburn still had 1:41 in which to win the game after LSU scored, but the defense preserved the 7-6 win.

LSU went on to win its seventh SEC title.

Perhaps there are times other than an LSU game when you've acted not quite like the sane, reserved, and responsible person you really are. The birth of your first child. Your wedding day. The concert of your favorite band. That fishing trip when you caught that big ole bass. You've probably been known to whoop it up pretty good when your emotions get the best of you.

But how many times have you ever let loose with a powerful shout to God in celebration of his love for you? Though God certainly deserves it, he doesn't require that you walk around waving pompoms and shouting "Yay, God!" He isn't particularly interested in having you arrested as a public menace.

No, God doesn't seek a big show or a spectacle. A nice little "thank you" is sufficient when it's delivered straight from the heart and comes bearing joy. That kind of shout carries all the way to Heaven; God hears it even if nobody else does.

Three SEC coaches I spoke with who have worked in other leagues say that Tiger Stadium is, by far, the loudest stadium in the country.
-- Bruce Feldman, ESPN.com

The shout of joy God likes to hear is a heartfelt
"thank you," even when it's whispered.

DAY 51

LIVE ACTION

Read James 2:14-26.

"Faith by itself, if it is not accompanied by action, is dead"
(v. 17).

Overly proud of Eastern football, a coach ran his mouth before a game with LSU about how the Southern boys didn't stand a chance. He had crow for supper that Saturday night.

The Tigers made their first-ever football road trip in 1894 by steamboat. In 1939, though, they became one of the first football teams to fly to a game. Coach Bernie Moore didn't like it at all, but the game was against Holy Cross in Worcester, Mass. "This is the only way to travel to a game far away from home and not keep the boys out of classes too long," Moore said.

Moore's trepidation wasn't helped any by senior guard Dave Bartram, an engineering student. He was seated next to the coach as the plane cruised along, and he pulled out a slide rule and started fiddling with it. A nervous Moore asked what he was doing. Bartram smiled brightly and explained: "Coach, I've just figured out that if the engines quit, it will take us 32 seconds to hit the ground."

Few of the players had ever been on a plane, and several were airsick. The barfers included senior end Ken Kavanaugh, who would become an Air Force pilot in World War II.

The Holy Cross coach regarded the LSU game as little more than a practice for his powerhouse team. He said he might start

TIGERS

his second team and bragged that his Eastern team would show those Southern boys the way football was supposed to be played.

Kavanaugh apparently recovered quite well from his bout of airsickness. He scored four touchdowns as LSU pulled off a major upset by winning 28-7. He had three scores on passes from sophomore tailback Leo Bird. The fourth touchdown was the most sensational. Also playing defense, Kavanaugh intercepted a Holy Cross lateral and went 80 yards for the score.

The Holy Cross coach did all the talking; the LSU Tigers did all the playing.

Talk is cheap. Consider your neighbor or coworker who talks without saying anything, who makes promise she doesn't keep, who brags about his own exploits, who can always tell you how to do something but never shows up for the work.

How often have you fidgeted through a meeting, impatient to get on with the work everybody is talking about doing? You know – just as that LSU football game showed against Holy Cross -- that speech without action just doesn't cut it.

That principle applies in the life of a person of faith too. Merely declaring our faith isn't enough, however sincere we may be. It is putting our faith into action that shouts to the world of the depth of our commitment to Christ. Just as Jesus' ministry was a virtual whirlwind of activity, so are we to change the world by doing.

Jesus Christ is alive; so should our faith in Him be.

Don't talk too much or too soon.

-- Bear Bryant

Faith that does not reveal itself in action is dead.

HANGING IN THERE

Read Mark 14:32-42.

"'Father,' he said, 'everything is possible for you. Take this cup from me. Yet not what I will, but what you will'" (v. 36).

With the season on the line, LSU's 2000 softball team was at its most futile, striking out 21 times and not scoring a run for 12 innings. But the Tigers persisted, refusing to fold, and won one of the most dramatic games in school history.

The Tigers met Southern Mississippi on May 20 in the NCAA Softball Regional at Tiger Park. An early loss meant the SEC champions had to win or their season was over. The challenge was a tough one as Southern Miss sent an All-American pitcher to the mound. The Tigers countered with 22-5 Ashley Lewis, and what resulted was "nearly 4 1/2 hours of unspeakable drama."

The innings slipped by: five, six, seven. And neither team had scored. Eight, nine, ten. Still no score. Eleven, twelve. Finally, the home-plate umpire asked Tiger catcher Jennifer Schuelke, "How long are you going to let this go?" Shuelke's answer illustrated the Tigers' resolve: "As long as it takes."

It took thirteen innings. In the top half, Schuelke led off by belting a double. Pinch runner Jennie Reeves took third on Stacey Newton's sacrifice bunt. Dee Douglass beat out an infield single to short, but Reeves stayed at third.

That brought up All-American second baseman Stephanie

TIGERS

Hastings. She came through, lifting a fly ball deep to left that chased Reeves home with the game's first and last run.

The drama wasn't over, though. The Golden Eagles loaded the bases with one out before Lewis managed to get a pair of strikeouts to end the marathon. The win was the team's 59th of the season, a new school record.

"Our intensity never failed," Lewis said. "All the defensive plays we made we never faltered." They persisted and they won.

Life is tough; it inevitably beats us up and kicks us around some. But life has four quarters, and so here we are, still standing, still in the game. Like the LSU softball team of 2000, we know that we can never win if we don't finish. We emerge as winners and champions only if we never give up, if we just see it through.

Interestingly, Jesus has been in the same situation. On that awful night in the garden, Jesus understood the nature of the suffering he was about to undergo, and he begged God to take it from him. In the end, though, he yielded to God's will and surrendered his own.

Even in the matter of persistence, Jesus is our example. As he did, we push doggedly and determinedly ahead – following God's will for our lives -- no matter how hard it gets. And we can do it because God is with us.

Both teams refused to lose. That was a whole year of sweat and blood.
– LSU softball coach Glenn Moore on the win over Southern Miss

It's tough to keep going no matter what,
but you have the power of almighty God
to pull you through.

BODY LANGUAGE

Read 1 Corinthians 6:12-20.

"Do you not know that your body is a temple of the Holy Spirit, who is in you, whom you have received from God? . . . Honor God with your body" (vv. 19, 20b).

Dalton Hilliard was just too small to be a running back at the major collegiate level.

The recruiters took one look at his size -- 5-foot-8, 185 lbs. -- and backed off. Everyone except LSU and Tulane. Even when Hilliard arrived in Baton Rouge in the fall of 1982, LSU's coaches questioned whether they should even play a man so small at running back. That's when linebacker coach Buddy Nix declared, "An offensive line opens holes that are wide, not high."

When the first depth chart of the fall was released showing Hilliard to be the No. 1 running back, most LSU fans believed Coach Jerry Stovall was pulling some kind of psychological ploy. But backfield coach Darrell Moody knew the chart was the truth. After all, he had told Stovall, "We've got a problem. Our third-string back (Hilliard at the time) is better than anyone we have."

What Hilliard did have was ability; he "seemed to glide into a hole, and then change speed and direction as if he weren't governed by the laws of physics." "People were wondering if Dalton was big enough to take the punishment," Nix said. "Nobody's had a clean tackle on him yet."

And then there were those thighs that at a glance seemed to

TIGERS

be "the size of most male waists." When a defender did get a rare clear shot at Hilliard, he ran into legs sturdy as pillars.

In the fall of 1982, Hilliard became the first freshman running back in modern Tiger history to draw the starting assignment. The "Little Big Man" went on to become LSU's all-time leading rusher and leading scorer and the ninth all-time receiver.

Turns out, Dalton Hilliard was plenty big after all.

Just like most of the so-called recruiting experts who considered Dalton Hilliard too small, most of us don't see a body beautiful when we look into a mirror. Too heavy, too short, too pale, too gray, and where'd all the hair go? We often compare ourselves to an impossible standard Hollywood and fashion magazines have created, and we are inevitably disappointed.

God must have been quite partial to your body, though, because he personally fashioned it and gave it to you free of charge. Your body, like everything else in your life, is thus a gift from God. But God didn't stop there. He then quite voluntarily chose to inhabit your body, sharing it with you in the person of the Holy Spirit. What an act of consummate ungratefulness it is then to abuse your God-given body by violating God's standards for living. To do so is in fact to dishonor God.

[Dalton Hilliard's doctor] said he'd never seen muscles like that, even in medical school.
    -- Jo Ann Landry, Hilliard's assistant high school principal

**You may not have a fine opinion of your body,
but God thought enough of it
to personally create it for you.**

WORK ETHIC

Read Matthew 9:35-38.

"Then he said to his disciples, 'The harvest is plentiful but the workers are few. Ask the Lord of the harvest, therefore, to send out workers into his harvest field'" (vv. 37-38).

After working out with him, his quarterback couldn't believe he was a major-college prospect he was so bad. And yet he left LSU as a two-time All-America and the greatest receiver in school history to that time. How to account for the change? Hard work.

Wendell Davis was not a hot prospect coming out of high school. LSU assistant coach Terry Lewis, who signed him, said, "He looked like a normal little guy." But Lewis spotted great athletic potential. When quarterback Tommy Hodson showed up and worked out some with Davis, he discovered Davis couldn't run under his long passes or catch his short ones. "I was not overly impressed," Hodson said.

But while Davis didn't possess the greatest raw athletic talent, he did have something else in abundance that more than made up for what he was missing. He had an incredibly strong work ethic. He worked tirelessly at catching footballs and running precise and disciplined routes. He worked on his hand-eye coordination. He got faster. He first began to make the routine catches, declaring "the patterns came before the hands." Then the difficult catches also began to stick to those hands.

When Hodson got the starting nod as a redshirt freshman in

TIGERS

1986, "he had a ready-made, polished target to throw to: Davis." The Tigers won the SEC in 1986, and Davis was named All-America in both '86 and '87. His 80 receptions in 1986 was a school record and led the nation. He also led the country that season with 11 touchdown catches. Davis left LSU as the school's and the SEC's all-time leading receiver in yardage. He was a first-round pick of the Chicago Bears and twice led the team in receiving.

And he worked hard for every pass he caught and every yard he gained.

Do you embrace hard work or try to avoid it? No matter how hard you may try, you really can't escape hard work. Funny thing about all these labor-saving devices like cell phones and laptop computers: You're working longer and harder than ever. For many of us, our work defines us perhaps more than any other aspect of our lives. But there's a workforce you're a part of that doesn't show up in any Labor Department statistics or any IRS records.

You're part of God's staff; God has a specific job that only you can do for him. It's often referred to as a "calling," but it amounts to your serving God where there is a need in the way that best suits your God-given abilities and talents

You should stand ready to work for God all the time, 24-7. Those are awful hours, but the benefits are out of this world.

My father is the person I thank for [my work ethic]. Football and other things came after my duties at home.
— *Wendell Davis*

God calls you to work for him using the talents and gifts he gave you; whether you're a worker or a malingerer is up to you.

THE LEADER

Read Matthew 16:13-19.

"You are Peter, and on this rock I will build my church, and the gates of Hades will not overcome it" (v. 18).

Here's a fine mess.

The head football coach was fired in midseason, and the whole team threatened to quit. Named interim coach, an assistant coach was on a boat to Cuba while the team played. The school then entered negotiations with the coach whose win had led to the firing before borrowing an assistant coach from another school. That was the situation in 1916 as LSU struggled to find a leader for its football team.

The day after a 7-0 loss to Sewanee, Coach E.T. McDonnell was fired, a move to which McDonnell responded by declaring, "I have played a square game here at LSU and I am not ashamed of my record." Indeed, his record was 14-7-1. Fans and players alike were outraged, the latter meeting to decide whether they would walk out for the rest of the season. McDonnell himself showed up at the team meeting and encouraged them to continue playing, which they did.

Assistant coach Irving Pray was asked to lead the team on a temporary basis. He was a sugar chemist, however, who had already obligated himself to sail for Cuba when the sugar-cane grinding season started. So athletic officials began negotiations with the Sewanee head coach, but they went nowhere.

TIGERS

Pray led the Tigers to a 17-7 win over Arkansas and then lit out for Cuba on the day the Tigers were to play Mississippi State. Scrambling officials managed to borrow Texas assistant coach Dana X. Bible to finish the season as head coach.

Every aspect of life that involves people – every organization, every group, every project, every team -- must have a leader. If goals are to be reached, somebody must take charge.

Even the early Christian church was no different. Jesus knew this, so he designated the leader in Simon Peter, who was, in fact, quite an unlikely choice to assume such an awesome, world-changing responsibility. In *Twelve Ordinary Men*, John MacArthur described Simon as "ambivalent, vacillating, impulsive, unsub-missive." Hardly a man to inspire confidence in his leadership skills. Yet, Peter became, according to MacArthur, "the greatest preacher among the apostles" and the "dominant figure" in the birth of the church.

The implication for your own life is obvious and unsettling. You may think you lack the attributes necessary to make a good leader for Christ. But consider Simon Peter, an ordinary man who allowed Christ to rule his life and became the foundation upon which the Christian church was built.

Would it not be worth trying to employ a man acquainted with Southern football, pay him a decent salary, and allow him to stay on the job long enough to see whether his system could be made successful?
-- Baton Rouge State-Times in the wake of McDonnell's firing

God's leaders are men and women
who allow Jesus to lead them.

A CHANGED LIFE

Read Romans 6:1-14.

"Just as Christ was raised from the dead through the glory of the Father, we too may live a new life" (v. 4).

Some players were surprised by what Coach Dale Brown did in the locker room on Dec. 10, 1988, after his lightly regarded LSU Tigers defeated highly ranked Florida on the road 111-101. He went down to one knee and led his team in prayer.

At that time in his life, prayer for the most successful coach in LSU basketball history was "as natural to him as if he had been alone at home in his study." Praying was such an important part of his daily life that the response was "almost automatic."

But it hadn't always been that way. In fact, since he had come to Baton Rouge in 1972 to replace Press Maravich, Brown "had not put much stock in praying with his team." Sometimes they prayed the Lord's Prayer, and that was about it. Usually, he just gave them time for silent prayer. He probably would have called any coach who prayed with his team a "fake." In an ESPN interview he had made it clear he didn't think much of his nickname, "Preacher Man," which referred to his coaching style.

Yet here in 1988, he not only was leading his team in prayer but had appointed a spiritual coach, who gave a short sermon before each game. Obviously, something had changed in Dale Brown's life. What had changed was the presence of Jesus.

His wife, Vonnie, had become seriously ill the previous summer,

TIGERS

and together they turned to God and committed their lives to Christ. "We're on a mission now," Vonnie told her husband, that went beyond basketball to getting others to turn to Christ.

The peace of Jesus in his life affected everything Brown did from the way he coached games, handled practices, and treated referees to the way he recruited and reached out to others.

Dale Brown was a changed man.

Anyone who asserts no change is needed in his or her life isn't paying attention. Every life has doubt, worry, fear, failure, frustration, unfulfilled dreams, and unsuccessful relationships in some combination. The memory and consequences of our past often haunt and trouble us.

Recognizing the need for change in our lives, though, doesn't mean the changes that will bring about hope, joy, peace, and fulfillment will occur. We need some power greater than ourselves or we wouldn't be where we are.

So where can we turn to? Where lies the hope for a changed life? It lies in an encounter with he who is the Lord of all Hope: Jesus Christ. For a life turned over to Jesus, change is inevitable. With Jesus in charge, the old self with its painful and destructive ways of thinking, feeling, loving, and living is transformed.

A changed life is always only a talk with Jesus away.

When everyone else is down on us, Coach Brown changes it all around. He is always lifting us up.
-- Ricky Blanton, first-team All-SEC (1988-89)

**In Jesus lie the hope and the power
that change lives.**

DAY 57

OLD-FASHIONED GUY

Read Leviticus 18:1-5.

"You must obey my laws and be careful to follow my decrees. I am the Lord your God" (v. 4).

The heart and soul of the offense of the 2007 national championship team was a throwback, an old-fashioned kind of football player who was named for a John Wayne character and who emerged like some ghost from the 1950s.

As *Sports Illustrated* put it, "Contemporary football players don't come much more retro than [Jacob] Hester, a married, hard-nosed runner." Among LSU fans who know something of the program's storied history, Hester was most often compared to All-American iron man Jim Taylor, a fullback and linebacker of the 1950s. Unlike Taylor, Hester didn't get the chance to play both ways, but he came mighty close. During the 2007 season, he showed up on kickoff coverage, punt coverage, punt return, and extra point and field goal teams. He also started at fullback, leading the national champions in rushing attempts, yards, and touchdowns while never fumbling once the entire season.

SI described Hester, who was named for the lead character in *Big Jake*, as "the consummate throwback player," one who preferred to get his yards the hard way, by pounding inside and going through tacklers rather than around them. "I guess I am a little bit of an oddball," Hester said about the way he played the game. "It's an honor being called an old-school player."

TIGERS

Hester's style wasn't all that was throwback about him; so was his appearance. He was a rarity in today's game: a white running back who was a great team's dominant rusher. Against Tennessee in 2006, Hester took off his headgear during a timeout, and a surprised Volunteer linebacker asked, "Shouldn't you be playing running back for Air Force?"

When LSU head coach Les Miles, sportswriters, and fans alike described Jacob Hester as "old-fashioned," they paid him a compliment. Usually, though, to refer to some person, some idea, or some institution as old-fashioned is to deliver a full-fledged insult. They're out of step with the times and the mores, hopelessly out of date, totally irrelevant, and quite useless.

For the people of God, however, "old-fashioned" is exactly the lifestyle we should pursue. The throwbacks are the ones who value honor, dignity, sacrifice, and steadfastness, who can be counted on to tell the truth and to do what they say. Old-fashioned folks shape their lives according to eternal values and truths, the ones handed down by almighty God.

These ancient laws and decrees are still relevant to contemporary life because they direct us to a lifestyle of holiness and righteousness that serves us well every single day. Such a way of living allows us to escape the ultimately hopeless life to which so many have doomed themselves in the name of being modern.

I guess I was born a little too late.

-- Jacob Hester

**The ancient lifestyle God calls us to still directs us
to a life of contentment, peace, and joy,
which never grows old-fashioned.**

ANSWERING THE CALL

Read 1 Samuel 3:1-18.

"The Lord came and stood there, calling as at the other times, 'Samuel! Samuel!' Then Samuel said, 'Speak, for your servant is listening'" (v. 10).

Joseph Barksdale wasn't too gung-ho about the suggestion he was met with the first day he arrived on campus. He bought into it, though, answered the call, and has never looked back.

In January 2007, Barksdale, one of the most highly recruited defensive tackles in the country, made his way to Baton Rouge from Michigan. He came south to be a star. His first day on campus he met new offensive line coach Greg Studrawa, who introduced himself by asking Barksdale if he had ever considered playing offensive line. "The answer wasn't even lukewarm." "He wasn't exactly gung-ho about the idea," Studrawa said.

Not only did Barksdale have visions of being a star wreaking havoc on opposing quarterbacks, he perceived offensive linemen as big, slow, and unathletic. "So, yeah, he balked at the idea at first," Studrawa said.

But there was a whole lot of talent on the defensive interior line at the time while on the other side of the ball, a host of freshmen were poised to battle for playing time at the right tackle spot. In short, the team needed Barksdale to step across the line.

Barksdale knew that head coach Les Miles was an old o-lineman himself, so when Miles talked, he listened. "When he talked to me about how good he thought I could be as an offensive lineman if I worked hard, it caught my attention," Barksdale said. With that final nudge from Miles, Barksdale made the move in the spring.

The first thing he learned was how wrong he had been about the athletic abilities of offensive linemen. "When you play defense, you get all the publicity for making a few plays," he said, but on offense, "You have to be consistent and can't take any plays off."

After answering the call, Barksdale played in every game in 2007 and started every game at right tackle in 2008 and 2009.

A team player is someone who does whatever the coach calls upon him to do for the good of the team. Something quite similar occurs when God places a specific call upon a Christian's life.

This is much scarier, though, than shifting positions on a football team as Joseph Barksdale did. The way many folks understand it is that answering God's call means going into the ministry, packing the family up, and moving halfway around the world to some place where folks have never heard of air conditioning, jambalaya, paved roads, or the LSU tigers. Zambia. The Philippines. Cleveland even.

Not for you, no thank you. And who can blame you?

But God usually calls folks to serve him where they are. In fact, God put you where you are right now, and he has a purpose in placing you there. Wherever you are, you are called to serve him.

I love being an offensive lineman now. This is where I was meant to be.
— Joseph Barksdale

God calls you to serve him right now
right where you are

CLOCKWORK

Read Matthew 25:1-13.

"Keep watch, because you do not know the day or the hour" (v. 13).

Paul Dietzel was such a stickler for organization, timing, and promptness that he didn't even operate in the same time zone as everyone else.

Dietzel coached the Tigers from 1955-'61, leading the team to the 1958 national championship. He left Baton Rouge with 46 wins, at the time the most in school history.

Among his players was Steve Ward, a linebacker and a three-year letterman from 1960-62. He said that under Dietzel, life was strictly regimented. "Everything we did at LSU was based on an itinerary with a time slot for everything," Ward said. "Every practice was timed to perfection."

Ward said the schedule for game day was so precise that a space on the itinerary allowed five minutes after pregame warmups for "NP." All the players knew this meant "Nervous Pee."

In August of 1961, Dietzel had a meeting scheduled for 1:05 p.m., which allowed the team 35 minutes to return to their rooms after lunch and review their playbooks. Ward dozed off and awoke at one o'clock. He sprinted downstairs, his heart pounding. At the door to the meeting room, he checked his watch: exactly 1:05. The door, however, was locked, so he "tapped on the door -- lightly."

Dietzel himself opened the door. "All 125 of my teammates

TIGERS

were sitting in their desks totally silent." Ward told Dietzel, "Coach, my watch shows it's 1:05." Ward said Dietzel looked at him "with those steel gray eyes" and said, "Son, I don't recognize your time. I operate on Central Dietzel Time and you're three minutes late. See me after this meeting."

Ward had to run three miles after practice for the next three days. "I was never late again for any of Coach Dietzel's meetings," he said.

We may pride ourselves on our time management, but the truth is that we don't manage time; it manages us. Hurried and harried, we live by schedules that seem to have too much what and too little when. By setting the bedside alarm at night, we even let the clock determine how much down time we get. A life of leisure actually means one in which time is of no importance.

Every second of our life – all the time we have – is a gift from God, who dreamed up time in the first place. We would do well, therefore, to consider what God considers to be good time management. After all, Jesus himself warned us against mismanaging the time we have.

From God's point of view, using our time wisely means being prepared at every moment for Jesus' return, which will occur -- well, only time will tell when.

To this day, I still set my watch three minutes ahead and operate on Central Dietzel Time.

– Steve Ward

**We mismanage our time
when we fail to prepare for Jesus' return
even though we don't know when that will be.**

TEARS IN HEAVEN

Read Revelation 21:1-8.

*"[God] will wipe every tear from their eyes. There will be
no more death or mourning or crying or pain" (v. 4).*

Yes, there is crying in baseball. The LSU Tigers revealed that
startling fact when they shed tears of joy after winning the 2000
College World Series in dramatic fashion.

The tears were part of the wild celebration that followed an
incredible comeback and a 6-5 win over Stanford that completed
the drive to the Tigers' fifth national championship. They became
the first team since 1978 to go undefeated in the entire postseason
and only the third team in NCAA history to win the championship in the bottom of the ninth.

Stanford led 5-2 and LSU hadn't had a hit since the second
inning when third baseman Blair Barbier slammed a solo homer
in the eighth to give the Tigers and their fans a lift. Designated
hitter Wally Pontiff walked and one out later, outfielder Jeremy
Witten slapped a game-tying homer.

Then in the bottom of the ninth, shortstop Ryan Theriot
singled and advanced on Mike Fontenot's walk. Catcher Brad
Cresse slapped a single to left to score Theriot. Cresse raised his
right arm with the No. 1 sign when he saw his hit clear the infield,
the tears starting before the winning run even scored. "I turned
and watched Theriot score," he said. "I was just standing there
between first and second" when the mob of delirious LSU players

TIGERS

came running out and launched "a dogpile celebration."

"Did that really just happen?" Theriot asked after he crossed home plate with the game-winning run and then began the celebration by throwing his batting helmet as far as he could.

An emotional Coach Skip Bertman eschewed the dogpile for a hug from outgoing athletic director Joe Dean. His eyes teary, Bertman said, "This may be the best ever." On this day when gritty Tiger players and their tough coaches cried.

When your parents died. When a friend told you she was divorcing. When you broke your collarbone. When you watch a sad movie.

You cry. Crying is as much a part of life as are breathing and indigestion. Usually our tears are brought on by pain, sorrow, or disappointment.

But what about when your child was born? When you discovered Jesus Christ? Those times elicit tears too; we cry at the times of our greatest, most overwhelming joy.

Thus, while there will be tears in Heaven, they will only be tears of sheer, unmitigated, undiluted joy. The greatest joy possible, a joy beyond our imagining, must occur when we finally see Christ. If we shed tears when LSU wins a game, can we really believe that we will stand dry-eyed and calm in the presence of Jesus?

What we will not shed in Heaven are tears of sorrow and pain.

This is the first time I'm tearless for more than a minute.
-- Jeremy Witten recovering from the dramatic win over Stanford

Tears in Heaven will be like everything else there:
a part of the joy we will experience.

CLOTHES HORSE

Read Genesis 37:1-11.

"Israel loved Joseph more than all his children, because he was the son of his old age: and he made him a coat of many colours" (v. 3 KJV).

Legendary LSU quarterback Y.A. Tittle is most certainly the only Tiger football player in history "to moon an opponent, in a losing cause, and still make the Hall of Fame."

Tittle's given name was Yelberton Abraham, but he asked LSU publicist Jim Corbett to "lay off using my name." Instead, Corbett recognized it "as football's most exciting name" and Tittle as the college game's "greatest T-formation passer and quarterback."

Tittle led the Tigers to 7-2, 9-1, and 5-3-1 seasons from 1945-47. The 1946 squad was ranked No. 8 in the nation and tied Arkansas 0-0 in the Cotton Bowl, the infamous "Ice Bowl" played in subfreezing temperatures and under sheets of snow and rain. Tittle is a member of the LSU Athletics Hall of Fame and the Pro Football Hall of Fame. The New York Giants retired his #14.

Against Ole Miss on Nov. 1, 1947, Tittle had a rather famous problem with his uniform. The Rebels were ahead 13-6 when Tittle, playing left corner on defense, intercepted a pass. The intended receiver managed only to reach back and make a seemingly futile grab at Tittle's midriff. "Between that slight tug in one direction and Tittle's momentum to the other, however, something had to give. It turned out to be Tittle's belt buckle."

TIGERS

Tittle suddenly faced the challenge of not only negotiating 70 yards of playing field through the Ole Miss players but doing it while cradling the ball with one hand and holding up his pants with the other. A Rebel player recalled, "I was racing down the field after him laughing and laughing. I couldn't help it; it was just the funniest thing I ever saw in football." Hemmed in on the sidelines, Tittle tried to stiff-arm a tackler, and his pants would have gone completely down if he hadn't.

Contemporary society proclaims that it's all about the clothes, though in Y.A. Tittle's case it was about the uniform. Buy that new suit or dress, those new shoes, and all the sparkling accessories, and you'll be a new person. The changes are only cosmetic, though; under those clothes, you're the same person. Consider Joseph, for instance, prancing about in his pretty new clothes; he was still a spoiled tattletale whom his brothers despised.

Jesus never taught that we should run around half-naked or wear only second-hand clothes from the local mission. He did warn us, though, against making consumer items such as clothes a priority in our lives. A follower of Christ seeks to emulate Jesus not through material, superficial means such as wearing special clothing like a robe and sandals. Rather, the disciple desires to match Jesus' inner beauty and serenity -- whether the clothes the Christian wears are the sables of a king or the rags of a pauper.

I'm not sure if I could have scored or not.
-- Y.A. Tittle on the effect of his pants problem

**Where Jesus is concerned,
clothes don't make the person; faith does.**

JUGGERNAUT

Read Revelation 20.

"Fire came down from heaven and devoured them. And the devil, who deceived them, was thrown into the lake of burning sulfur, where the beast and the false prophet had been thrown" (vv. 9b-10a).

They were one of the greatest juggernauts college football had ever seen. "On paper, they appeared to be almost unbeatable," at least by LSU. But when the Bayou Bengals played Oklahoma on Jan. 4, 2004, "records would fall, legends would be made and the LSU Tigers would become national champions."

LSU was just another team living in Oklahoma's mighty shadow during the 2003 football season. The Sooners were ranked No. 1 all season long. They led the nation in scoring behind Heisman-Trophy winner Jason White. They had the top-ranked defense.

The Sooners were so confident that playing LSU was a mere formality they had to endure before their coronation that the university's Web site featured national championship merchandise -- before the game. "It's difficult in a situation like this," Coach Nick Saban said before the game, "but we've got a good football team and that's how we want to play."

The problem for the Sooners was that despite all their gaudy statistics and all the fawning of the media, they hadn't played LSU. Yet. When they did, the juggernaut turned out to be the team wearing purple and gold.

TIGERS

The juggernaut started rolling on the game's first play when freshman tailback Justin Vincent -- the game's MVP -- took a handoff and sprinted 64 yards to the OU 16. The Tigers ultimately fumbled, but the handwriting was on the wall: LSU was not afraid and Oklahoma should be.

The game was tied at seven when LSU marched eighty yards on that supposedly impregnable defense with Vincent getting the last 18. The Tigers would never trail again in winning 21-14.

Maybe your experience with a juggernaut involved a game against a team full of major college prospects, a league tennis match against a former college player, or your presentation for the project you knew didn't stand a chance. Whatever it was, you've been slam-dunked before.

Being part of a juggernaut is certainly more fun than being in the way of one. Just ask LSU's opponents in 2003 and again in 2007. Or consider the forces of evil aligned against God. At least the teams that took the field against the Tigers in those national championship seasons had some hope, however slim, that they might win. No such hope exists for those who oppose God.

That's because their fate is already spelled out in detail. We all know how the story ends. God's enemies may talk big and bluster now, but they will be trounced in the most decisive defeat of all time. You sure want to be on the winning side in that one.

Early in the season, prognosticators were comparing them to some of the great college teams of all time.

> -- Tiger Terrific *on the Oklahoma Sooners*

**The most lopsided victory in all of history is a
sure thing: God's ultimate triumph over evil.**

DOWNRIGHT CRAZY

Read Luke 13:31-35.

"Some Pharisees came to Jesus and said to him, 'Leave this place and go somewhere else. Herod wants to kill you.' He replied, 'Go tell that fox . . . I must keep going today and tomorrow and the next day'" (vv. 31-33).

What LSU head basketball coach Dale Brown proposed to do was downright crazy. What he did, however, turned out to be downright shrewd, giving Tiger fans one of the most bizarre and exciting games in school history.

On Feb. 3, 1990, Loyola Marymount traveled across the country to play the Tigers. LMU was in essence the freak show of college basketball. They played a breakneck style of run-and-gun, seeking to get a shot up in four or five seconds. They were so good at it that that they were ranked No. 20 in 1990 despite giving up 108 points a game. They didn't care; they averaged 121.

SEC teams had no experience with anything like LMU. The logical approach would have been to try to slow them down. Brown didn't see it that way. He liked the pace of LMU's play; he wanted to run with them and whip them at their own game.

It sounded crazy. But Brown looked at his star-studded lineup that included Chris Jackson and twin towers Shaquille O'Neal and Stanley Roberts and figured his team could match up with LMU. The result was a classic before more than 14,000 LSU fans who showed up "with an almost morbid curiosity to see the

Marymount toy, sort of like gawkers at the state fair lining up to see the three-headed calf."

The points came . . . and they came. The scoring was so fast that official scorer Al Toups gave up trying to watch the action and instead listened to the PA announcer so he could keep up. Late in the first half, an electric typewriter used to record play-by-play in this day before computers literally caught fire when the motor burned up.

The exhausting game went into overtime before LSU got the lead and finally slowed the pace down. The Tigers won 148-141.

What some see as crazy often is shrewd instead. Like the time you went into business for yourself or when you decided to go back to school. Maybe it was when you fixed up that old house. Or when you bought that new company's stock.

You know a good thing when you see it but are also shrewd enough to spot something that's downright crazy. Jesus was that way too. He knew that his entering Jerusalem was in complete defiance of all apparent reason and logic since a whole bunch of folks who wanted to kill him were waiting for him there.

Nevertheless, he went because he also knew that when the great drama had played out he would defeat not only his personal enemies but the most fearsome enemy of all: death itself. It was, after all, a shrewd move that provided the way to your salvation.

Crazy like a fox.
-- One writer's description of Brown's decision to run with LMU

It's so good it sounds crazy -- but it's not: through faith in Jesus, you can have eternal life with God.

AMAZING!

Read: Luke 4:31-36.

"All the people were amazed and said to each other, 'What is this teaching? With authority and power he gives orders to evil spirits and they come out!'" (v. 36)

Chad Jones' 93-yard punt return that supplied the winning touchdown was amazing enough, but LSU fans for decades will be shaking their heads in amazement at what the defense did against Mississippi State.

Jones' return on the first play of the fourth quarter gave the No. 7 Tigers a 30-21 lead against the Bulldogs on Sept. 26, 2009. But State was far from through. A field goal made it 30-24, and the Starkville boys got the ball at midfield with 3:53 left to play. They promptly ripped off yardage in huge chunks until an 18-yard romp gave them a first and goal at the LSU two.

With the clock running down, now was the time for head coach Les Miles to consider a strange but legitimate option: Let State score. The Tigers would have more than a minute for quarterback Jordan Jefferson and the offense to kick a field goal for the win. After the game, Miles said he never considered it. He put his trust in his defense; the results were amazing.

Senior defensive tackle Al Woods stopped State on first down but only inches away from the goal line. Woods struck again on second -- still inches from a game-winning touchdown.

On third down, State tried a play-action pass, but the Tigers weren't fooled. Incredibly, Jones made another play, swatting the pass away after instructing the linebackers to watch the run.

That left fourth and inches. State went to the fullback, and linebacker Kelvin Sheppard hit him right away. Backup linebacker Ryan Baker then hit him low, and Jones finished one of the most amazing goal-line stands in history by knocking him backward.

The word *amazing* defines the limits of what you believe to be plausible or usual. The Grand Canyon, the birth of your children, those last-minute goal-line stands and bone-crunching defensive plays -- they're amazing! You've never seen anything like that before!

Some people in Galilee felt the same way when they encountered Jesus. Jesus amazed them with the authority of his teaching, and he wowed them with his power over spirit beings. People everywhere just couldn't quit talking about him.

It would have been amazing had they not been amazed. They were, after all, witnesses to the most amazing spectacle in the history of the world: God himself was right there among them walking, talking, teaching, preaching, and healing.

Their amazement should be a part of your life too because Jesus still lives. The almighty and omnipotent God of the universe seeks to spend time with you every day – because he loves you. Amazing!

It's amazing. Some of the greatest characteristics of being a winning football player are the same ones it's true to be a Christian man.
-- Bobby Bowden

Everything about God is amazing,
but perhaps most amazing of all is that he loves us
and desires our company.

DAY 65

THE PRIZE

Read Philippians 3:10-16.

"I press on toward the goal to win the prize for which God has called me heavenward in Christ Jesus" (v. 14).

College football players receive various types of accolades, prizes, and awards every season, but an LSU player once refused an honor the likes of which has probably never been offered since: He was to be made a Louisiana state senator!

LSU halfback "Miracle" Abe Mickal led the Tigers to a 23-4-5 record from 1933-35. He went on to a career in the NFL and was inducted into the College Football Hall of Fame in 1967.

His passing ability was legendary in a day when the ball was rounder than today's pigskin and thus was much more difficult to grasp and heave with anything resembling precision. In 1934, he teamed with fellow Hall of Famer Gaynell Tinsley on a last-ditch 65-yard touchdown pass that tied SMU 14-14. The play was the longest scoring pass in Southern football history; their record stood for several years.

Louisiana Gov. Huey Long was such a fan of Mickal's that he often visited practice and helped him take off his jersey. He created a stir by proposing to make Mickal a state senator. LSU Coach Biff Jones was furious. He protested to his athletic director, Red Heard, that making such a spectacle of one player was bad for morale and was interfering with the team. When Long heard of the coach's sentiments, he proposed to make state senators of the whole team.

Mickal refused to report for his installation. Eventually, Heard was able to put a stop to the whole mess by pointing out to Long that if he were made a state senator, Mickal would probably be ruled ineligible for football. The $10 per diem paid to state senators would jeopardize Mickal's amateur standing.

Even the most modest and self-effacing among us can't help but be pleased by prizes and honors. They symbolize the approval and appreciation of others, whether it's an honorary title, an Employee of the Month trophy, a plaque for sales achievement, or the sign declaring yours as the neighborhood's prettiest yard.

Such prizes and awards are often the culmination of the pursuit of personal achievement and accomplishment. They represent accolades and recognition from the world. Nothing is inherently wrong with any of that as long as we keep them in perspective.

That is, we must never let awards become such idols that we worship or lower our sight from the greatest prize of all and the only one truly worth winning. It's one that won't rust, collect dust, or leave us wondering why we worked so hard to win it in the first place. The ultimate prize is eternal life, and it's ours through Jesus Christ.

Maybe they ought to try making something of their senators.
-- Will Rogers on being told Louisiana was trying to make senators
of its football players

**The greatest prize of all doesn't require
competition to claim it; God has it ready
to hand to you through Jesus Christ.**

HOMEBODIES

Read 2 Corinthians 5:1-10.

"We . . . would prefer to be away from the body and at home with the Lord" (v. 8).

The Tigers once played a home game 1,400 miles from Baton Rouge.

Along with everyone else, in September 2005 the LSU football team endured "a fortnight of the chaos and sorrow that flowed into Baton Rouge along with the thousands of evacuees in the aftermath of Hurricane Katrina." Thus, the Bayou Bengals started their season two weeks later than originally scheduled. To get that season under way, though, the Tigers had to travel to Tempe, Ariz., to play what everyone had expected to be their second home game of the season.

Why would they do such a thing? Because the shell-shocked folks in Louisiana needed something to cheer about, and the Tigers gave them a chance to do just that. "We wanted to win for our fans," said senior wide receiver Skyler Green, who called New Orleans home and who for two weeks had not only shared his two-bedroom apartment with his roommate, offensive lineman Brian Johnson, but also with displaced relatives and friends.

The Sun Devils of Arizona State were the epitome of gracious hosts for the displaced Tigers. They helped pay the Tigers' meal and travel costs to ensure the bulk of the game's proceeds would go toward hurricane relief. They allowed the Tigers to wear their customary white home jerseys and to enter the stadium after they did. The hotel in which the Tigers stayed even managed to add grits to the breakfast menu.

Playing with heavy hearts against a team that had already won a game, the Tigers fell behind 17-7 after three quarters. "We were not going to give up," quarterback JaMarcus Russell declared. The fourth quarter was wild with the lead changing hands four times. Finally, on fourth and 10 with 1:23 left, Russell hit wideout Early Doucet with a game-winning 39-yard touchdown pass.

Far from home, the Tigers won for the home folks 35-31.

Home is not necessarily a matter of geography. It may be that place you share with your spouse and your children, whether it's Louisiana or Arizona. You may feel at home when you return to Baton Rouge, wondering why you were so eager to leave in the first place. Maybe the home you grew up in still feels like an old shoe, a little worn but comfortable and inviting.

God planted that sense of home in us because he is a God of place, and our place is with him. Thus, we may live a few blocks away from our parents and grandparents or we may relocate every few years, but we will still sometimes feel as though we don't really belong no matter where we are. We don't; our true home is with God in the place Jesus has gone ahead to prepare for us. We are homebodies and we are perpetually homesick.

Everybody's better at home.
— *Basketball player Justin Dentmon*

**We are continually homesick for our real home,
which is with God in Heaven.**

DREAM WORLD

Read Joel 2:26-28.

"Your old men will dream dreams, your young men will see visions" (v. 28).

The stuff of dreams. Many call it the greatest single moment in LSU athletic history. But less than two months before Warren Morris' dramatic home run, he wasn't sure he would ever play baseball again.

"It was the very sort of dream every kid has while playing baseball in the backyard," Morris said. With two out in the bottom of the ninth of the championship game of the 1996 College World Series, Morris hit the first pitch he saw into the right-field stands for a two-run homer, a 9-8 LSU win, and the national title.

For Morris, the dream had come true. Much of the 1996 season, however, had been a nightmare for him. He was a pre-season All-America at second base. Eleven games into the season, though, he hurt a hand. He sat out a month and tried to come back, but the pain was worse than before. He sat out another month.

Morris called that time "the lowest point in my baseball career." The worst part of all was that no one could diagnose his injury. "It seemed to be one of those mysterious ailments that bring an end to a career. I wasn't sure I would be able to play again."

So one night Morris dropped to his knees and prayed: "God, if baseball is what You want me to do in life, then I will do it and give all the glory to You." But if you have something else in mind,

"I'll do it and serve You in that way."

Two days later, a doctor discovered Morris had a broken bone. He had surgery and soon was playing again. The wrist injury limited his power, however, so he was dropped into the bottom of the lineup. He had not hit a home run all season -- until the day every kid's dream came true for Warren Morris.

You have dreams. Maybe to make a lot of money. Write the great American novel. Or have the fairy-tale romance. But dreams often are crushed beneath the weight of everyday living; reality, not dreams, comes to occupy your time, attention, and effort. You've come to understand that achieving your dreams requires a combination of persistence, timing, and providence.

But what if your dreams don't come true because they're not good enough? That is, they're based on the alluring but totally unreliable promises of the world rather than the true promises of God, which are a sure thing.

God calls us to great achievements because God's dreams for us are greater than our dreams for ourselves. Such greatness occurs, though, only when our dreams and God's will for our lives are the same. Your dreams should be worthy of your best – and worthy of God's involvement in making them come true.

An athlete cannot run with money in his pocket. He must run with hope in his heart and dreams in his head.
-- Olympic Gold Medalist Emil Zatopek

Dreams based on the world's promises
are often crushed; those based on God's promises
are a sure thing.

PRECIOUS MEMORIES

Read 1 Thessalonians 3:6-13.

"Timothy . . . has brought good news about your faith and love. He has told us that you always have pleasant memories of us" (v. 6).

Chase Pittman remembered. That was why he couldn't follow in his brother's footsteps.

Chase was a junior in high school, and his brother Cole was a football player for the Texas Longhorns on his way back to Austin for spring practice when he was killed in a single-car accident on Feb. 26, 2001. "It didn't seem real," Chase said. "Sometimes it still doesn't seem real."

Chase did what seemed natural: He followed in his brother's footsteps to Texas. But his brother's constant presence wore on him. Texas had honored Cole by preserving his locker. Chase "was just two lockers down from a perpetual reminder of just how empty his heart felt." "We had talked about playing with each other at Texas," Chase said, "and seeing his locker kept reminding me that it was never going to happen."

So despite a bright future at Texas, Chase left and came to LSU after the 2003 season. He sat out the 2004 season and then started every game for the Tigers at defensive end in 2005 and 2006. For Chase, LSU was a perfect fit. He was a key part of the SEC's best defensive line in 2005. And, too, he could remember Cole in his own way. Over his heart, he had a tattoo that read "Cole P" and the date of his birth and death. He also wore a wrist band with No. 44 -- Cole's number - on it.

"I think about him every day, every thirty minutes, every 10 minutes, all the time," Chase said. "He's never too far away."

Your whole life will one day be only a memory because – hold your breath for this red-hot news flash -- you will die. With that knowledge in hand, you can get busy and make some preparations for that fateful day by selecting a funeral home, purchasing a cemetery plot and picking out your casket or opting for cremation and choosing a tasteful urn, designating those who will deliver your eulogy, and even making other less important decisions about your send-off.

What you cannot control about your death, however, is how you will be remembered and whether your demise leaves a gaping hole in the lives of those with whom you shared your life or a pothole that's quickly paved over. What determines whether those nice words someone will say about you are heartfelt truth or pleasant fabrications? What determines whether the tears that fall at your death result from heartfelt grief or a sinus infection?

Love does. Just as Paul wrote, the love you give away during your life decides whether or not memories of you will be precious and pleasant.

Whenever I walk out of the tunnel at Tiger Stadium, I'm thinking about him.

– Chase Pittman on his brother, Cole

**How you will be remembered after you die
is largely determined by how much
and how deeply you love others now.**

ANIMAL MAGNETISM

Read Psalm 139:1-18.

"For you created my inmost being; you knit me together in my mother's womb. I praise you because I am fearfully and wonderfully made" (vv. 13-14).

Mike the Tiger is probably the most awesome and the most admired mascot in the country. But LSU could easily have become known as the Pelicans, which certainly isn't nearly as fearsome.

LSU's first football mascot, in fact, was a greyhound. In 1896, "Drum," the pet of the school's commandant of cadets, served as the football team's mascot. That same squad also underwent a growing identification with the pelican as the players had pelican insignia sewn on their jackets.

Almost from the first team in 1893, though, the tiger was associated with LSU football. As the 1896 season wore on, the team gradually became to be more and more known as the Tigers. The reference was probably to the Seventh Louisiana Infantry of the Army of Northern Virginia. They were a particularly ferocious bunch that often charged with Bowie knives and returned from battle wearing necklaces made from Yankee body parts.

The first live cat mascot was a jaguar, introduced in 1924. Nicknamed "Little Eat 'Em Up," the cat was not a great success since he reportedly turned his back on the action and cowered when LSU was about to score. It didn't help his reputation that the 1924 team didn't win a single game. He quickly disappeared from sight.

TIGERS

LSU zealots used papier-mache Tigers as symbols of school spirit during the 1920s and '30s until Mike Chambers, a football trainer, suggested a live mascot. The students quickly rallied around the idea. In an hour a fundraiser netted the $750 needed to purchase a cub from the Little Rock Zoo in 1936. Originally named "Sheik," the Tiger's name was changed to "Mike" to honor the instigator of the whole idea.

Today, Mike VI reigns regally over his LSU kingdom.

Animals such as Mike elicit our awe and our respect. Nothing enlivens a trip more than glimpsing turkeys, bears, or deer in the wild. Admit it: You go along with the kids' trip to the zoo because you think it's a cool place too. All that variety of life is mind-boggling. Who could conceive of a Bengal or a Siberian tiger, a walrus, a moose, or a prairie dog? Who could possibly have that rich an imagination?

But the next time you're at an LSU game or in a crowd, look around at the faces. Who could come up with the idea for all those different people? For that matter, who could conceive of you? You are unique, a masterpiece who will never be duplicated.

The master creator, God Almighty, is behind it all. He thought of you and brought you into being. If you had a manufacturer's label, it might say, "Lovingly, fearfully, and wonderfully handmade in Heaven by #1 -- God."

We wanted a mascot that could stand up and roar.
-- Jack Fiser, LSU student, on support for a live tiger in 1936

You may consider some painting
or a magnificent animal a work of art,
but the real masterpiece is you.

DRY RUN

Read John 4:1-15.

*"Everyone who drinks this water will be thirsty again,
but whoever drinks the water I give him will never thirst.
Indeed, the water I give him will become in him a spring
of water welling up to eternal life" (vv. 13-14).*

The drought was of biblical proportions. It lasted twelve years.

On Nov. 6, 1982, LSU ended twelve years of bondage with a 20-10 defeat of Alabama. For eleven seasons in a row, Bear Bryant and the Tide had owned LSU; not since a 14-9 win in Birmingham in 1970 by Charlie McClendon's SEC champions had LSU won.

That drought ended, though, with the deliverance directed by an unlikely Moses, "a feeble-looking, yet heady player named Alan Risher, who orchestrated miracle after miracle with his right arm and wiggly feet." The senior quarterback completed twenty passes and scrambled continually for yardage to lead No. 10 LSU to victory over the seventh-ranked Tide.

LSU Coach Jerry Stovall called it "without a doubt, the biggest victory I've ever had as a coach," which was pretty heady seeing as how the Tigers had earlier defeated fourth-ranked Florida. "You can't understand what it's like to get hit in the mouth 11 years in a row." Bryant called it "the best beating we've had since the 1960's."

LSU took command of the game with seventeen points in the second quarter. Dalton Hilliard had a 16-yard TD run, Risher

TIGERS

hit Malcolm Scott with a 3-yard scoring toss, and Juan Carlos Betanzos kicked a 23-yard field goal. Meanwhile, the nation's top-ranked rushing defense held the Tide to 32 total yards and no first downs in the half and only 45 yards rushing all day.

Alabama rallied in the third quarter to cut the lead to 17-10, but LSU answered with a 63-yard, 13-play drive that took almost six minutes off the clock and ended with a field goal.

The drought was over.

You can walk across that river you boated on in the spring. The city's put all neighborhoods on water restriction, and that beautiful lawn you fertilized and seeded will turn a sickly, pale green and may lapse all the way to brown. Somebody wrote "Wash Me" on the rear window of your truck.

The sun bakes everything, including the concrete. The earth itself seems exhausted, just barely hanging on. It's a drought.

It's the way a soul looks that shuts God out.

God instilled thirst in us to warn us of our body's need for physical water. He also gave us a spiritual thirst that can be quenched only by his presence in our lives. Without God, we are like tumbleweeds, dried out and windblown, offering the illusion of life where there is only death.

Living water – water of life – is readily available in Jesus. We may drink our fill, and thus we slake our thirst and end our soul's drought – forever.

This ends twelve years of suffering as a fan and player.
-- Alan Risher after the 1982 win over Alabama

Our soul thirsts for God's refreshing presence.

A GENTLE MAN

Read John 2:13-22.

"He made a whip out of cords, and drove all from the temple area . . .; he scattered the coins of the money changers and overturned their tables" (v. 15).

Harry Rabenhorst was "a great model of a Christian gentleman, showing by his actions how to live a happy, productive, responsible life."

So spoke Benny McArdle, who played both basketball and baseball for Rabenhorst, one of the legends of LSU sports history.

"Coach Raby" arrived in Baton Rouge in 1925. His main coaching responsibilities were basketball and baseball, but he also served as an assistant football coach for eighteen years. Except for a three-year stint in the Navy in World War II, he coached every LSU baseball and basketball team from 1925-57. He served as both LSU's assistant athletic director and athletic director, retiring in 1968.

Rabenhorst won 344 basketball games at LSU, the school record subsequently broken by Dale Brown. He won what was then the mythical national championship in 1934-35. As a baseball coach, he won two SEC titles.

Through all the ups and downs, "Coach Raby" "was the most pure Christian-type person you'd ever want to meet in life," said a relative who played basketball at LSU. Rabenhorst was "a man of integrity and sound moral principles." He never cheated, would never ask a professor to change a student's grade, and expected all "his boys" to play by the rules.

So how could such a gentleman be so successful? He was a strict disciplinarian. He once left a baseball player in Mississippi because he didn't get to the bus on time after the team stopped for lunch though the player came running after the departing bus.

A calm, caring manner and a soft voice are often taken for weakness, and gentle men are frequently misunderstood by those who fail to appreciate their inner strength. But Harry Rabenhorst's coaching career and Jesus' rampage through the Jerusalem temple illustrate the perils of underestimating a determined gentleman.

A gentleman treats other people kindly, respectfully, and justly, and conducts himself ethically in all situations. A gentleman doesn't lack resolve or backbone. Instead, he determines to live in a way that is exceedingly difficult in our selfish, me-first society; he lives the lifestyle God desires for us all.

Included in that mode of living is the understanding that the best way to have a request honored is to make it civilly, with a smile. God works that way too. He could bully you and boss you around; you couldn't stop him. But instead, he gently requests your attention and politely waits for the courtesy of a reply.

I have never known a coach with more humility and gentle feelings toward his players than Coach Raby.

-- *Coach Charles McClendon*

**God is a gentleman, soliciting your attention
politely and then patiently waiting for you
to give him the courtesy of a reply.**

NIGHTFALL

Read Psalm 68:12-23.

*"The day is yours, and yours also the night; you
established the sun and moon" (v. 16).*

Ladies and gentlemen, it's Saturday night in Death Valley, and
here come your Fighting Tigers of LSU." With those words, yet
another team prepares to meet its fate.

Night football in Tiger Stadium began with the season opener
in 1931. The idea was the brainchild of T.P. "Skipper" Heard, who
was then the graduate manager of athletics and later was the
athletics director (1932-55).

Several reasons have traditionally been cited for the decision:
avoiding the heat and humidity of afternoon games, avoiding
scheduling conflicts with Tulane and Loyola, and giving more
fans the chance to see the Tigers play. The evening contest caught
the public's fancy immediately, a newspaper feature writer
describing it as a "nocturnal spectacle in which the game assumed
an aspect delightfully theatrical."

The tradition was continued probably because of an immediate
and consistent increase in attendance, though that was not the
case at that first night game on Oct. 3, 1931. It rained.

The opponent was Spring Hill, so it wasn't a major game to
begin with. Fearing the worst because of the weather, admin-
istrators lowered the ticket prices to virtual giveaway levels.
Reserved sideline seats were $1.50; end zone bleacher seats were

TIGERS

only 75 cents. High school students got in for a quarter; grammar students could see the game for one thin dime.

The promotion didn't work as only about 5,000 fans braved the elements to watch LSU win 35-0.

That win became the norm as the Tigers have consistently played better at night than they have during the day. The faithful fanatics have certainly bought into the tradition, making Saturday night in Death Valley "the freakiest, funkiest, most frenetic place in all of college football."

A rarity in 1931, night football has become an accepted part of contemporary college football. With the lighting expertise we have today, our night games are played under conditions that are "as bright as day."

It is artificial light, though, manmade, not God-made. Our electric lights can only illumine a portion of God's night; they can never chase it away. The night, like the day, is a gift from God to be enjoyed, to function as a necessary part of our lives. The night is a part of God's plan for creation and a natural cycle that includes activity and rest.

The world is different at nightfall. Whether we admire a stunning sunset, are dazzled by fireflies, or simply find solace in the descending quiet, the night reminds us of the variety of God's creation and the need the creation has for constant renewal.

Dracula and LSU football are at their best after the sun goes down.
-- ESPN's Beano Cook

**Like the day, night is part of both
the beauty and the order of God's creation.**

A LONG SHOT

Read Matthew 9:9-13.

"[Jesus] saw a man named Matthew sitting at the tax collector's booth. 'Follow me,' he told him, and Matthew got up and followed him" (v. 9).

The most decorated LSU football player since Billy Cannon was a long shot even to walk, let alone play outdoors.

After the 2007 national championship game, Ohio State right tackle Kirk Barton called Glenn Dorsey "one of the most impressive players I've ever seen." That's probably not praise enough for the defensive tackle others had called the best player in college football on either side of the ball. In addition to being named All-America for the second time, Dorsey in 2007 as a senior won the Nagurski Award as the nation's best defensive player, the Lombardi Award as the best lineman or linebacker, and the Outland Trophy as the country's best interior lineman.

He was an imposing sight at 6'2" and 303 pounds. A close look, though, revealed the evidence of the experience that fueled Dorsey's unrelenting drive. He still has a slight bow to his legs, a reminder and a remnant of a time when he couldn't even walk.

In 1988, 3-year-old little Glenn Dorsey was so bowlegged that doctors told his mother his legs would not straighten on their own. His legs were so bowed and misshaped that he couldn't walk, continually tripping over his own feet.

So his mother had him fitted with corrective shoes and ankle-high braces connected by a bar. The result was a painful memory, not necessarily of the braces, but of their effect. They meant little Glenn had to sit on the sideline while his friends played. "I was on the porch, just watching everybody," Dorsey recalled. He took a football to bed at night and dreamed of playing.

By age 8, though, his legs were straight enough for him to play. And Glenn Dorsey, the long shot, because Glenn Dorsey the star.

Matthew the tax collector was another long shot, an unlikely person to be a confidant of the Son of God. While we may not get all warm and fuzzy about the IRS, our government's revenue agents are nothing like Matthew and his ilk. He bought a franchise, paying the Roman Empire for the privilege of extorting, bullying, and stealing everything he could from his own people. Tax collectors of the time were "despicable, vile, unprincipled scoundrels."

And yet, Jesus said only two words to this lowlife: "Follow me." Jesus knew that this long shot would make an excellent disciple.

It's the same with us. While we may not be quite as vile as Matthew was, none of us can stand before God with our hands clean and our hearts pure. We are all impossibly long shots to enter God's Heaven. That is, until we do what Matthew did: get up and follow Jesus.

To know where he's come from and to know where he's at now -- it's like a miracle to me.
-- Sandra Dorsey, mother of Glenn

**Only through Jesus does our status change
from being long shots to enter God's Kingdom
to being heavy favorites.**

THE BIG TIME

Read Matthew 2:19-23.

"He went and lived in a town called Nazareth" (v. 23).

Sue Gunter made the trek from the backwoods to the big time.

The population of Walnut Grove, Miss., is officially listed at 394. The community sports a bank and three highways. The Kansas City Southern railway runs through town. The nearest airport is sixty miles away in Jackson; it has no international flights.

There in the Mississippi backwoods Gunter grew up playing sports. Her favorite was basketball, which she played constantly with her cousins on the family farm not just because she enjoyed it but also because there really wasn't anything else to do. In Walnut Grove, "if you were going to be popular, you better play basketball. Or at least learn to dribble."

She dribbled her way out of Walnut Grove, all the way to Montreal and the 1976 Olympics as an assistant coach for the USA women's basketball team. She made stops at Middle Tennessee State and Stephen F. Austin before she arrived in Baton Rouge in 1982. And there she hit the big time.

Her first season she led the Lady Tigers to a 20-7 record and was named National Coach of the Year. She went on to win 442 games in 22 seasons before health forced her to retire in 2004. Overall, she won 708 games in forty seasons, the third most in women's basketball history. She was inducted into the Naismith Basketball Hall of Fame in 2005.

TIGERS

Perhaps Gunter's biggest dream of all came true in 2003 when LSU hosted Tennessee before nearly 15,000 fans, a throng so huge that the fire marshal had to step in. "Sue had tears in her eyes that day," LSU legend Skip Bertman said. Selling out the PMAC "was always something she dreamed about and it came true that day."

There in the big time, a long way from Walnut Grove.

The move to the big time is one we often desire to make in our own lives. Bumps in the road, one-stoplight communities, and towns with only a service station, a church, and a voting place litter the American countryside. Maybe you were born in one of them and grew up in a virtually unknown village in a backwater county. Perhaps you started out on a stage far removed from the bright lights of Broadway, the glitz of Hollywood, or the halls of power in Washington, D.C.

Those original circumstances don't have to define or limit you, though, for life is much more than geography. It is about character and walking with God whether you're in the countryside or in the city.

Jesus knew the truth of that. After all, he grew up in a small town in an inconsequential region of an insignificant country ruled by foreign invaders.

Where you are doesn't matter. What you are does.

I live so far out in the country that I have to walk toward town to go hunting.

-- Former Major Leaguer Rocky Bridges

**Where you live may largely be the culmination
of a series of circumstances;
what you are is a choice you make.**

DAY 75

GOOD-BYE

Read John 13:33-38.

"My children, I will be with you only a little longer" (v. 33a).

What if they threw a good-bye party and the honoree wouldn't go away? That's what happened with old Alex Box Stadium.

On Sunday, May 11, 2008, LSU whipped Mississippi State 9-6 in the last game scheduled at The Box. The 70-year-old ballpark was to make way for a new stadium, then under construction.

For many, it was an emotional day, full of the fond memories of a lifetime. Snapshots were taken. "Husbands and wives hugged, held hands and embraced" after the game. Some had met or dated at the venerable stadium. "Couples just don't spend Mother's Day at a college baseball game because they can't think of anything better to do." They were there to say good-bye to an old friend.

Athletic Director Skip Bertman peeled the last piece off the stadium countdown sign. It now read "0 Games Remaining at the Box." The current Tigers joined more than 100 former players in a postgame lap around the field, slapping hands with the fans.

All in all, it was a lovely good-bye party. A hint, though, that The Box might not go away so quietly came when Bertman asked the fans not to scoop up infield dirt or rip out seats and carry the ballpark away bit by bit. He suspected The Box might have one last run in it. So did his wife, Sandy, who placed a small sign over the countdown zero that said "NCAA Still to Come!"

TIGERS

They were right. Two weeks later, the word came down that the stadium would host an NCAA baseball regional tournament. That would be it, right? Well, no. On the longest winning streak in SEC baseball history (ultimately 23 games), the Tigers swept the regional, and The Box wound up hosting a super regional.

Finally -- and fittingly -- on June 9 the Tigers and their fans bid the stadium good-bye with a 21-7 romp over UC-Irvine that sent LSU to Omaha and the College World Series.

You've stood on the curb and watched someone you love drive off, or you've grabbed a last-minute hug before a plane leaves. Maybe it was a child leaving home for the first time or your best friends moving halfway across the country. It's an extended – maybe even permanent – separation, and good-byes hurt.

Jesus felt the pain of parting too. Throughout his brief ministry, Jesus had been surrounded by and had depended upon his friends and confidantes, the disciples. About to leave them, he gathered them for a going-away supper and gave them a heads-up about what was about to happen. In the process, he offered them words of comfort. What a wonderful friend he was! Even though he was the one who was about to suffer unimaginable agony, Jesus' concern was for the pain his friends would feel.

But Jesus wasn't just saying good-bye. He was about his mission of providing the way through which none of us would ever have to say good-bye again.

It was a tremendous facility in its day.
– Major League Scout Leon McGraw on the old Alex Box Stadium

Through Jesus, we will see the day
when we say good-bye to good-byes.

PLAN AHEAD

Read Psalm 33:1-15.

"The plans of the Lord stand firm forever, the purposes of his heart through all generations" (v. 11).

Extensive and meticulous planning is required for any football team's road trip, but sometimes the most careful planning goes awry. For instance, the Tigers once got caught with no way to get home from a bowl game.

Many colleges dropped their football programs altogether during World War II. LSU was among only four SEC schools -- Tulane, Georgia, and Georgia Tech were the others -- that fielded a team in 1943. The shorthanded Tigers nevertheless managed to compile a 6-3 record and received an Orange Bowl bid, partly because the bowls had so few teams from which to choose. "All we hoped to do when the season started was keep football alive," Coach Bernie Moore admitted, expressing his surprise about the invitation. The opponent was Texas A&M, which had beaten the Tigers 28-13 during the season.

Moore told reporters he was optimistic about LSU's chances in the bowl game because star tailback Steve Van Buren, nagged by injuries during the season, was healthy. That was enough. Van Buren rushed for 160 yards, scored two touchdowns and passed to Burt Goode for the third as LSU won 19-14.

Then came the glitch in the planning for the trip. The Tigers couldn't get home. No rail accommodations were available, and

TIGERS

seats on commercial airplanes weren't a consideration in the middle of the war. Lewis Gottlieb, the student manager in 1915, stepped forward and bailed the team out in a most unusual way.

A banker, Gottlieb owned a car dealership in Baton Rouge. He contacted a fellow dealer in Miami with whom he had done business and bought enough used cars for the team to drive home in. He then put the cars on his lot and sold them.

Successful living takes planning. You go to school to improve your chances for a better paying job. You use blueprints to build your home. You plan for retirement. You map out your vacation to have the best time. You even plan your children -- sometimes.

Like LSU's 1943 trip to the Orange Bowl, your best-laid plans, however, sometimes get wrecked by events and circumstances beyond your control. The economy goes into the tank; a debilitating illness strikes; a hurricane hits. Life is capricious and thus no plans -- not even your best ones -- are foolproof.

But you don't have to go it alone. God has plans for your life that guarantee success as God defines it if you will make him your planning partner. God's plan for your life includes joy, love, peace, kindness, gentleness, and faithfulness, all the elements necessary for truly successful living for today and for all eternity. And God's plan will not fail.

I don't remember what the cars were except I bought a Cadillac for Bernie to come home in because he won the game, and I wanted him to travel in style.

-- Lewis Gottlieb

**Your plans may ensure a successful life;
God's plans will ensure a successful eternity.**

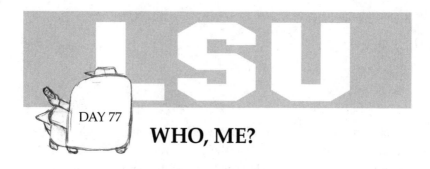

WHO, ME?

Read Judges 6:11-23.

"'But Lord,' Gideon asked, 'how can I save Israel? My clan is the weakest in Manasseh, and I am the least in my family'" (v. 15).

Coach Nick Saban gave Rohan Davey the surprise of his life, and the result was an LSU win in the 2000 Peach Bowl.

"I wasn't even thinking I might be going in," Davey said as halftime came. There really was no reason for him to think he might be playing. The starter was Josh Booty, the All-SEC quarterback. Davey hadn't taken a single snap in five and a half games. But with the Bayou Bengals behind Georgia Tech 14-3 at the break and with an offense that had managed only 117 yards the first half, Saban turned to Davey and to his surprise turned the game over to him.

"The seemingly almost-forgotten backup" did quite well. "He comes in the huddle in the third quarter, and it was like turning on a light switch," said safety Ryan Clark.

Davey was five-of-five passing for 57 yards as he led the Tigers on a 70-yard scoring drive. His last pass went to fullback Tommy Banks for a touchdown. Three possessions later, Davey was at it again, taking the Bayou Bengals 53 yards and completing three of four tosses for 26 yards. On third and goal from the Tech nine, Davey eluded a rush and then fired a bullet to Josh Reed in the back of the end zone. LSU had the lead for good.

TIGERS

Davey finished his remarkable night 17 of 25 passing for 174 yards and three touchdowns -- in only thirty minutes of play.

Explaining the decision to change quarterbacks, offensive coordinator Jimbo Fisher said, "What we needed was an emotional lift, and Ro was our emotional leader." His value to the team was illustrated when the players after the season voted Rohan their permananent offensive captain. Saban said he had never before had a team when the honor went to a backup player.

You probably know exactly how Rohan Davey felt; you've experienced that moment of surprise with its sinking "who, me?" feeling. How about that time the teacher called on you when you hadn't done a lick of homework? Or the night the hypnotist pulled you out of a room full of folks to be his guinea pig? You've had the wide-eyed look and the turmoil in your midsection when you were suddenly singled out and found yourself in a situation you neither sought nor were prepared for.

You may feel the same way Gideon did about being called to serve God in some way, quailing at the very notion of being audacious enough to teach Sunday school, lead a small group study, or coordinate a high school prayer club. After all, who's worthy enough to do anything like that?

The truth is that nobody is – but that doesn't seem to matter to God. And it's his opinion, not yours, that counts.

Surprise might not be the right word. I was more than just surprised.
-- Rohan Davey on being inserted into the 2000 Peach Bowl.

**You're right in that no one is worthy to serve God,
but the problem is that doesn't matter to God.**

CHEERS

Read Matthew 21:1-11.

"The crowds that went ahead of him and those that followed shouted" (v. 9).

Softball coach Yvette Girouard made sure Kristin Schmidt ended her career with one final curtain call. The crowd obliged, allowing Schmidt to exit to the cheers of a standing ovation.

The crowd cheered not just for the end of a great career but for one of the most remarkable displays of tenacity and will in LSU athletic history. The three-time All-America had just thrown 20 2/3 consecutive innings -- in one day -- to help the Tigers twice stave off elimination in the 2004 Women's College World Series. The Tiger senior would later be named the series MVP.

When the day began at 10 a.m., LSU faced elimination with a single loss. Schmidt intended to pitch two games and yield to freshman Emily Turner for the final game. She threw a four-hit masterpiece with 13 strikeouts in the first game to whip FSU. She then whipped Cal 4-1, yielding only seven hits to set up another showdown with Cal for the right to advance to the national title game against UCLA.

After 34 innings and 513 pitches in the World Series, Schmidt thought her work was through. But Girouard wanted her best lineup on the field, and that meant Schmidt. "I saw her do it in summer ball, but to see her do it at the World Series . . . wow," said senior second baseman Sara Fitzgerald. Schmidt's comment

TIGERS

was, "I was willing to pitch as long as coach would let me. . . . I'm probably never going to play softball again, so I might as well just give it everything that's in me." She carried a 1-0 lead into the fifth inning before a controversial call on a bunt led to four Cal runs and the 4-1 score that was to hold up.

With two outs in the top of the seventh, Girouard made her move, fully expecting that the knowledgeable crowd would give Schmidt the cheers she deserved.

Chances are you go to work every day, do your job well, and then go home to your family. This country couldn't run without you; you're indispensable to the nation's efficiency. Even so, nobody cheers for you or waves pompoms in your face. Your name probably will never elicit a standing ovation when a PA announcer calls it.

It's just as well, since public opinion is notoriously fickle. Consider what happened to Jesus. When he entered Jerusalem, he was the object of raucous cheering and an impromptu parade. The crowd's adulation reached such a frenzy they tore branches off trees and threw their clothes on the ground. Five days later the crowd shouted again, only this time they screamed for Jesus' execution.

So don't worry too much about not having your personal set of cheering fans. Remember that you do have one personal cheerleader who will never stop pulling for you: God.

Kudos to our sport because this young lady certainly deserved that.
— Yvette Girouard on Kristen Schmidt's standing ovation

**Just like the sports stars, you do have
a personal cheerleader: God.**

HEAD GAMES

Read Job 28.

"The fear of the Lord -- that is wisdom, and to shun evil is understanding" (v. 28).

Tiger head football coach Bernie Moore spent so much time thinking about football that he developed a well-deserved reputation for absentmindedness.

Only Charles McLendon (18 seasons) had a longer tenure as LSU head coach than Moore (13 seasons, 1935-'47). He won 83 games and coached the Tigers to their first five bowl games. He was also a highly successful track coach at LSU, winning the NCAA championship in 1933. LSU's outdoor track facility is named the Bernie Moore Stadium.

Moore had a sharp mind that frequently drifted off into the X's and O's of football. He would several times each morning wander out of his office, grab whoever might be standing around, and say, "Let's go get a little sip of coffee." At a drug store across campus, "Moore would lose himself in deep thought as he sipped about one-third of a cup of coffee." Then, still thinking about football, he often literally got lost on the way back to the office. His passengers usually just went along quietly for the meandering ride, knowing not to interrupt their coach's thoughts.

Once Moore asked a student assistant to write a letter for him. He started dictating but then stopped, gazing out a window and losing himself in thoughts about football. The student waited until Moore finally turned around, saw him sitting there, and said in surprise, "Good morning, son. What can I do for you?"

A standing joke was that the groundskeeper had to replant the grass in front of the LSU bench every season because Moore ate it. During a game, he paced constantly, frequently stooping to pick up a blade of grass and unconsciously sticking it between his teeth. Nobody ever saw him swallow it.

You're a thinking person. When you talk about using your head, you're speaking as Bernie Moore used his: Logic, reason, and careful thinking are part of your psyche. A coach's bad call frustrates you and your children's inexplicable behavior flummoxes you. Why can't people just think things through?

That goes for matters of faith too. Jesus doesn't tell you to turn your brain off when you walk into a church or open the Bible. In fact, when you seek Jesus, you seek him heart, soul, body, and mind. The mind of the master should be the master of your mind so that you consider every situation in your life through the critical lens of the mind of Christ. With your head *and* your heart, you encounter God, who is, after all, the true source of wisdom.

To know Jesus is not to stop thinking; it is to start thinking divinely.

Football is more mental than physical, no matter how it looks from the stands.
                              -- Pro Hall-of-Fame linebacker Ray Nitschke

**Since God is the source of all wisdom,
it's only logical that you encounter him
with your mind as well as your emotions.**

DAY 80

UNEXPECTEDLY

Read Luke 2:1-20.

"She gave birth to her firstborn, a son. She wrapped him in cloths and placed him in a manger, because there was no room for them in the inn" (v. 7).

The experts knew exactly how the SEC Championship Game of 2001 was going to turn out. LSU just didn't give them the game they expected.

Tennessee entered the game with a 10-1 record, a No. 2 national ranking, and a ticket to the national championship game in Miami if they won. The team was packed with a roster of future NFL stars, so the experts figured the Volunteers would meet only token resistance from the Tigers, whom, they said, had managed to "sneak" into the championship game with a 5-3 conference record thanks to some favorable tiebreakers.

Nobody bothered to tell the Tigers they didn't belong even after starting quarterback Rohan Davey and starting tailback LaBrandon Toefield went down with injuries. Matt Mauck and Domanick Davis simply stepped up to lead the Tigers to a 24-17 lead early in the fourth quarter.

But Tennessee moved to a first down at the Tiger four as Tiger cornerback Randall Gay limped off the field with a twisted ankle. Head coach Nick Saban had to turn to freshman Travis Daniels, who had not played a down all season long.

After an incomplete pass on first down, the Vols went right for

TIGERS

Daniels with a quick slant at the goal line. Unexpectedly, in only his second down of college football, Daniels was there to break up the pass. Another pass was incomplete on third down, and the Vols blinked. They opted for a field goal.

LSU scored again and Tennessee didn't. With a 31-20 win, the Tigers were unexpectedly the SEC champs.

Just like the experts who didn't give LSU a chance in 2001, we think we've got everything figured out and planned for, and then something unexpected happens. Someone gets ill; you fall in love; you lose your job; you're going to have another child. Life surprises us with its bizarre twists and turns.

God is that way too, catching us unawares to remind us he's still around. A friend who hears you're down and stops by, a child's laugh, an achingly beautiful sunset -- unexpected moments of love and beauty. God is like that, always doing something in our lives we didn't expect.

But why shouldn't he? There is nothing God can't do. The only factor limiting what God can do is the paucity of our own faith.

We should expect the unexpected from God, this same deity who unexpectedly came to live among us as a man. He does, by the way, expect a response from you.

Sports is about adapting to the unexpected and being able to modify plans at the last minute.
— Sir Roger Bannister, first-ever sub-four-minute miler

God does the unexpected -- like showing up
as Jesus -- to remind you of his presence,
and now he expects a response from you.

THE OUTER LIMITS

Read Genesis 18:1-15.

"Is anything too hard for the Lord?" (v. 14a).

What the LSU men's basketball team of 1999-2000 did was impossible, given the circumstances. They just didn't believe it.

As the season began, the LSU basketball program was in a "six-year soaking in the depths of an ocean of defeat." It didn't look like the program was going to surface anytime soon. After all, the Tigers were on probation that had left them with scholarship limitations. The season before they had won only four SEC games after winning only two conference games the season before that.

So maybe a winning season was an outside possibility. A bid to the National Invitational Tournament wasn't really probable, but it was a worthwhile goal. Anything more than that -- don't count on it.

So what did third-year coach John Brady's team do? They won 28 games and were champions of the Western Division and conference co-champions. They also defeated Southeast Missouri State and Texas to advance to the Sweet Sixteen in the NCAA Tournament. This "couldn't be a dream," one sportswriter said. "Dreams aren't this good." Or this unlikely.

But it's true. Led by forward Stromile Swift and center Jabari Smith, the squad nobody believed in or expected anything of put together one of the greatest seasons in LSU roundball history.

Swift may have been the only person who wasn't surprised

TIGERS

by the season. He chose to play for LSU because, while he knew nothing of scholarship limitations, he believed the coaching staff would get the talent in Baton Rouge necessary to win.

Probably even he didn't expect to win so quickly.

You've probably never tried a whole bunch of things you've dreamed about doing at one time or another. Like starting your own business. Going back to school. Campaigning for elected office. Running a marathon.

But what holds you back? Perhaps you hesitate because you see only your limitations, both those you've imposed on yourself and those of which others constantly remind you. But maybe as the LSU's men's basketball team did in 1999-2000, it's time you ignored what everybody says. Maybe it's time to see yourself the way God does.

God sees you as you are and also as you can be. In God's eyes, your possibilities are limitless. The realization of those latent possibilities, however, depends upon your depending upon God for direction, guidance, and strength. While you may quail in the face of the challenge that lies before you, nothing is too hard for the Lord.

You can free yourself from that which blights your dreams by depending not on yourself but on God.

If I would have told you this was going to happen last October, you would have laughed me out of town.
-- Sportswriter Sam King on the 1999-2000 LSU men's basketball team

Pray like everything depends upon God;
work like everything depends upon you

COMEBACK KIDS

Read Acts 9:1-22.

*"All those who heard him were astonished and asked,
'Isn't he the man who raised havoc in Jerusalem among
those who call on this name?'" (v. 21)*

One first down. Thirty-eight yards total offense. 13-0 deficit. That was the situation at halftime for the Tigers in the 1968 Sugar Bowl. And then they pulled a comeback.

After thirty minutes of football in New Orleans on Jan. 1, 1968, LSU looked like the underdog it was to the sixth-ranked and undefeated Wyoming Cowboys. But head coach Charlie McClendon made some changes at halftime that fueled a ferocious comeback and a storied Tiger victory.

With half a dozen reserves in the lineup to start the last half, the Tigers got back into the game by driving 80 yards for a touchdown. Sophomore tailback Glenn Smith put some spark into the Bengal offense, which had been totally dominated the first half. He finished with 74 yards rushing, averaging 4.7 yards a carry, and he capped the 80-yard drive with a plunge from the one. He would be named the game's Most Valuable Player.

After the defense forced a Cowboy punt, the Tigers moved relentlessly down the field again, keeping their comeback alive by marching 52 yards to tie the game. Quarterback Nelson Stokley hit end Tommy Morel with an eight-yard scoring toss. with 11:39 left in the game. The extra point was no good, leaving the teams knotted at 13.

All the momentum belonged to the Tigers, however, and the defense chipped in with a big play. Senior linebacker Benny Griffin intercepted his second Cowboy pass of the day and returned the theft to the Wyoming 31. Smith burst off right end for 16 yards before Stokley and Morel hooked up again, this time from 13 yards out with only 4:32 left in the game.

On the game's final play, LSU completed the last-half comeback by stopping Wyoming at the five-yard line.

Life will have its setbacks whether they result from personal failures or from forces and people beyond your control. Being a Christian and a faithful follower of Jesus Christ doesn't insulate you from getting into deep trouble. Maybe financial problems suffocated you. A serious illness put you on the sidelines. Or great tragedy struck your family. Life is a series of victories and defeats. Winning isn't about avoiding defeat; it's about getting back up to compete again. It's about making a comeback of your own.

When you avail yourself of God's grace and God's power, your comeback is always greater than your setback. You are never too far behind, and it's never too late in life's game for Jesus to lead you to victory, to turn trouble into triumph. As it was with the Tigers in the 1968 Sugar Bowl and with Paul, it's not how you start that counts; it's how you finish.

It's not where you're picked but where you finish.
-- Former LSU men's basketball coach John Brady

In life, victory is truly a matter of how you finish
and whether you finish with Jesus at your side.

DAY 83

STAR POWER

Read Luke 10:1-3, 17-20.

"The Lord appointed seventy-two others and sent them two by two ahead of him to every town and place where he was about to go" (v. 1).

A shot at the SEC championship and the national title was in their sights, but first the Tigers of 2003 had to defeat a team with a true star.

LSU was 9-1 and ranked third in the nation on Nov. 22 when the Tigers traveled to Oxford to play 15th-ranked Ole Miss, led by its star quarterback, Eli Manning. The pregame hype billed the game as "a marquee matchup between one of the nation's most heralded quarterbacks and one of the nation's stingiest defenses."

The defense won -- on both sides of the ball as the game was low scoring. The Ole Miss defense -- and not Manning -- got the game's first touchdown on an interception return on LSU's first play from scrimmage. Chris Jackson's 45-yard field goal cut the gap to four, and then with less than three minutes left in the first half, quarterback Matt Mauck hit receiver Michael Clayton with a nine-yard touchdown toss. LSU led 10-7 at the break.

The Tiger defense continued to shut Manning down through a scoreless third quarter. On the first play of the final period, Mauck and Devery Henderson teamed up for a 53-yard scoring toss. LSU led 17-7, and the way the defense was playing, that would be enough points for the win.

TIGERS

It was, but just barely as Manning finally got something going. Ole Miss moved 76 yards to make it a 17-14 thriller with 10:51 left. The Rebels then had three chances to tie or win the game, but each time the Tiger defense shut down the Ole Miss star.

"The quarterback is the starter and finisher for the offense," said defensive end Marcus Spears after the game. "If you get to him, . . . it makes a difference." Even when he's a star.

Football teams are like other organizations in that they may have a star but the star would be nothing without the supporting cast. It's the same in a government bureaucracy, a private company, a military unit, and just about any other team of people with a common goal.

That includes the team known as a church. It may have its "star" in the preacher, who is – like the quarterback or the company CEO – the most visible representative of the team. Preachers are, after all, God's paid, trained professionals.

But when Jesus assembled a team of seventy-two folks, he didn't have anybody on the payroll or any seminary graduates. All he had were no-names who loved him. And nothing has changed. God's church still depends on those whose only pay is the satisfaction of serving and whose only qualification is their love for God. God's church needs you.

You may have the greatest bunch of individual stars in the world, but if they don't play together, the club won't be worth a dime.
— Babe Ruth

**Yes, the church needs its professional clergy,
but it also needs those who serve as volunteers
because they love God; the church needs you.**

FEAR FACTOR

Read Matthew 14:22-33.

"[The disciples] cried out in fear. But Jesus immediately said to them: 'Take courage! It is I. Don't be afraid'" (vv. 26-27).

Just a routine day at LSU baseball practice running the bases when suddenly Greg Smith knew fear.

During the fall of 2002, Smith, a freshman pitcher, was running the bases as he had countless times before. Suddenly, though, his heart started beating very fast. "I waited for it to slow down," he said. He went home to his apartment and collapsed into his recliner. After several hours, the rapid heartbeat finally stopped, but Smith was exhausted. "I couldn't even get up to take a shower. I was so tired."

He knew what had happened wasn't normal. "Have you ever seen those cartoons where Bugs Bunny will see Lola, and his heart will beat through his chest?" he asked. "That's what it [was] like. If I lifted up my shirt, you could actually see my chest moving, beating real fast."

The next day LSU trainer Shawn Eddy and head coach Smoke Laval agreed their pitcher should see a doctor right away. Smith did indeed have a heart condition, a declaration by the cardiologist that of course scared Smith and his family. The problem wasn't serious enough to be life-threatening, however; in fact, he could continue playing baseball after undergoing a pair of procedures to lessen the problem.

So Smith came back to the team for the 2002 season, slightly fearful about a heavy workload being detrimental to his health. The only problem Smith had, however, was with the two-mile run. "Oxygen can't get to the muscles," he said, "and I get tired faster." His condition never interfered with his pitching.

After that fearful time, he went on to be first-team All-SEC in 2005, get drafted, and make his major league debut in 2008.

Some fears are universal; others are particular. Speaking to the Rotary Club may require a heavy dose of antiperspirant. Elevator walls may feel as though they're closing in on you. And don't even get started on being in the dark with spiders and snakes during a thunderstorm.

We all live in fear, and God knows this. Dozens of passages in the Bible urge us not to be afraid. God isn't telling us to lose our wariness of oncoming cars or big dogs with nasty dispositions; this is a helpful fear God instilled in us for protection. What God does wish driven from our lives is a spirit of fear that dominates us, that makes our lives miserable and keeps us from doing what we should, such as sharing our faith. In commanding that we not be afraid, God reminds us that when we trust completely in him, we find peace that calms our fears.

It scared the heck out of us.
> — *Greg Smith's father on his son's heart condition*

You have your own peculiar set of fears,
but they should never paralyze you
because God is greater than anything you fear.

STRANGE BUT TRUE

Read 1 Corinthians 1:18-31.

*"The message of the cross is foolishness to those who are
perishing, but to us who are being saved it is the power of
God" (v. 18).*

The game wasn't even played in the United States, the opposing team chugged wine during pregame warm-ups, and a chief
component of the game plan consisted of making an opposing
player throw up. Such went perhaps the strangest football game
in LSU history.

In 1907, the LSU Tigers became the first American football team
to play a game on foreign soil when they accepted an invitation
to play the University of Havana on Christmas Day. The Cubans
apparently wanted to play a legitimate American college team to
validate their team and bolster its reputation. What bothered LSU
coach Edgar Wingard most before the game was the island hospi-
tality. Every time the Tigers ran into other Americans, "they were
treated to drinks and a food spread," especially a dish of stewed
chicken and saffron rice.

During their warm-ups, the Tigers espied a rather strange
display on the Cuban bench: a long row of drinking glasses, each
filled with wine. Before the game, the Cuban players frequently
ran over and gulped some of the fruit of the vine.

LSU's great George "Doc" Fenton noticed that a 300-pound
lineman who had been recruited just to handle LSU's sensational

TIGERS

guard W.M. Lyles was among the most frequent imbibers. Fenton told Lyles, "Hit that guy in the stomach with your head and he's done for." Sure enough, "Lyles drew a bead" on the player's stomach and "fired right in." Fenton said, "The big guy sprouted like an artesian well. . . . We nearly had to swim out of there."

Fenton led a 56-0 rout in a strange, strange football game.

Life is just strange, isn't it? How else to explain the college bowl situation, Dr. Phil, tattoos, curling, tofu, and teenagers? Isn't it strange that today we have more ways to stay in touch with each other yet are losing the intimacy of personal contact?

And how strange is it that God let himself be killed by being nailed to a couple of pieces of wood? Think about that: the creator and ruler of the entire universe suffering the indignity and the torture that he did. And he did it quite willingly; this was God, after all. It's not like he wasn't capable of changing the course of events -- but he didn't. Isn't that strange?

But there's more that's downright bewildering. The cross, a symbol of disgrace, defeat, and death, ultimately became a worldwide symbol of hope, victory, and life. That's really strange.

So is the fact that love drove God to that cross. It's strange – but it's true.

It may sound strange, but many champions are made champions by setbacks.
-- Olympic champion Bob Richards

It's strange but true: God allowed himself to be killed on a cross because of his great love for you.

A LEVEL PLAYING FIELD

Read Romans 3:21-26.

"There is no distinction, since all have sinned and fall short of the glory of God" (vv. 22b-23 NRSV).

They played on the same field we did. That was pretty much LSU coach Gaynell Tinsley's response to assertions from North Carolina that the Tigers had pulled a dirty trick by watering down the football field.

It sure looked suspicious. Not a drop of rain had fallen for some time; yet when the teams began their warmups on Oct. 22, 1949, the Tiger Stadium field was definitely wet -- very wet. "Everybody from North Carolina," especially the Tar Heel coaches, regarded the water as a trick to slow down Carolina's all-world runner Charlie "Choo Choo" Justice. The Heels were unbeaten in twenty straight regular-season games and came into Baton Rouge a prohibitive favorite. Excessively watering the grass was an attempt by LSU to level the playing field, or so UNC claimed.

Tinsley knew he hadn't set any nefarious scheme into motion, so he did a little detective work and provided an explanation. A groundskeeper always watered the field the night before a home game, but since UNC wanted to work out at Tiger Stadium, Tinsley told the groundskeeper to go home and not worry about it. However, after the workout a diligent Tiger manager realized the field had not been watered and proceeded to do it. The next morning, the groundskeeper, not knowing the field had been watered, also quite diligently got the hoses going until Tinsley showed up and stopped him.

Whether it was a little too much water or not, the Tigers pulled off the upset 13-7 in what many considered at the time LSU's greatest football victory ever. Halfback Jim Roshto ran 27 yards for one score, and big fullback Zollie Toth scored the game-winner from one yard out, capping an 82-yard drive.

We should face up to one of life's basic facts: Its playing field isn't level. Others, it seems, get all the breaks. They get the cushy job; they win the lottery; their father owns the business. Some people – perhaps undeservedly -- just have it made.

That said, we just have to accept that the playing field isn't level and get over it. Dwelling on life's inequities can create only bitterness and cynicism, leading us to grumble about what we don't have while ignoring the blessings God continuously showers upon us. A moment's pause and reflection is all it takes for us to call to mind any number of friends, acquaintances, and strangers with whom we would not exchange situations.

The only place in life where we really stand on a level playing field is before God. There, all people are equal because we all need the lifeline God offers through Jesus — and we all have access to it.

Both teams played on the same field, and the only player who slipped on the field that night was LSU's Zollie Toth.
-- LSU Coach Gaynell Tinlsey on charges of leveling the playing field

Unlike life's playing field, God's playing field
is level because everyone has equal access
to what God has done through Jesus Christ.

FATHERS AND SONS

Read Matthew 3:13-17.

"A voice from heaven said, 'This is my Son, whom I love; with him I am well pleased'" (v. 17).

Before there was the Pistol, there was Press.

When Peter Press Maravich was born in 1947, his father, Press, announced the birth at halftime of a semipro basketball game. "This boy would do what the father could not": He would make a living playing basketball.

As Pete grew up around the high-school teams Press coached, "if you saw Press, you saw Pete." As an assistant coach put it, Pete "always wanted to be around Press, but Press was always around basketball." "The game was an obsession, but also a kind of love. Press worshipped basketball. Pete worshipped Press." Press' team would meet at the gym for away games, and the father would leave the son in the gym with the lights on with a one-word order: "Play." When the team returned home, "usually between midnight and one in the morning, Pete would still be there, still shooting."

In 1955, Press took the head coaching job at Clemson. He showed off his son during gatherings at his home. Nine-year-old Pete would dribble on concrete with gloves on and then blindfolded. Coaching legend John Wooden once asked his colleague about all the tricks and suggested the boy would be better off learning proper footwork for defense. "You don't understand," Press replied. "He's going to be the first million-dollar pro."

TIGERS

In all, Press came up with about forty drills and exercises for his son. They called them Homework Basketball, and as Pete got older, Press invented more elaborate regimens to hold his son's interest. Together, Press and Pete Maravich "worked at the edge of art and science" to produce what they called "Showtime." They also created a legend who played the game like no one before.

American society largely belittles and marginalizes fathers and their influence upon their sons. Men are perceived as necessary to effect pregnancy; after that, they can leave and everybody's better off.

But we need look in only two places to appreciate the enormity of that misconception: our jails – packed with males who lacked the influence of fathers in their lives as they grew up -- and the Bible. God – being God – could have chosen any relationship he desired between Jesus and himself, including society's approach of irrelevancy. Instead, the most important relationship in all of history was that of father-son.

God obviously believes a close, loving relationship between fathers and sons is crucial. For men and women to espouse otherwise or for men to walk blithely and carelessly out of their children's lives constitutes disobedience to the divine will.

Simply put, God loves fathers. After all, he is one.

My dad was a huge influence on me. I imagine if he had put a wrench in my hand I would have been a great mechanic.
*   -- Pete Maravich*

**Fatherhood is a tough job, but a model
for the father-child relationship is found
in that of Jesus the Son with God the Father.**

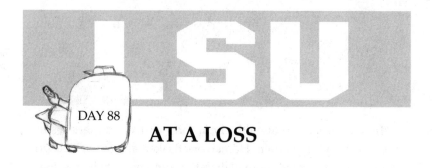

AT A LOSS

Read Philippians 3:7-11.

"I consider everything a loss compared to the surpassing greatness of knowing Christ Jesus my Lord, for whose sake I have lost all things" (v. 8).

Lord, what do we do now? Please guide my decision. It is in Your hands now."

Such was the prayer of LSU Athletic Director Paul Dietzel at a time when the Tiger football program was hit with a sudden loss that was "terrible," that devastated the coaching staff, and that drew chaos near. Such was Dietzel's prayer in the wake of the sudden and stunning death of football coach Bo Rein.

With Charlie McClendon's tenure as head Tiger ending after the 1979 season, Dietzel spent more than a year searching for a successor. He found him in Rein, 34, the four-year head coach at North Carolina State. Rein brought energy with him to Baton Rouge in December. He was a tireless recruiter, literally logging thousands of miles for LSU in 42 days. That's how long he was the Tiger head coach.

On Jan. 9, 1980, Rein and his pilot were flying home from a recruiting trip. Something happened. The plane veered off course, and attempts to establish radio contact failed. Eventually, more than 1,000 miles off course, the plane crashed into the Atlantic, presumably out of fuel.

"The tragedy rocked LSU to the foundations," and the loss of

TIGERS

the head coach threatened to throw the football program into chaos. With recruiting at its peak, Dietzel and Chancellor Paul W. Murrill had no time for an extensive search. Moreover, the school had obligations to McClendon's staff until June and to Rein's staff for a year. They couldn't afford to hire another established coach and his assistants and pay three staffs.

The solution was two-time LSU All-American Jerry Stovall, the man who could best minimize the effects of the loss.

Maybe, it was when a family member died as it was for the Tiger family at Bo Rein's death. Perhaps it wasn't so staggeringly tragic: your puppy died, your best friend moved away, or an older sibling left home. Sometime in your youth or early adult life, though, you learned that loss is a part of life.

Loss inevitably diminishes your life, but loss and the grief that accompanies it are part of the price of loving. When you first encountered loss, you learned that you were virtually helpless to prevent it or escape it.

There is life after loss, though, because you have one sure place to turn. Jesus can share your pain and ease your suffering, but he doesn't stop there. Through the loss of his own life, he transformed death -- the ultimate loss -- into the ultimate gain of eternal life. In Jesus lies the promise that one day loss itself will die.

I would gladly surrender this job, and any other, and my right arm if Bo Rein could still be here.
-- Jerry Stovall, upon being named LSU head football coach

Jesus not only eases the pain of our losses but transforms the loss caused by death into the gain of eternal life.

PAIN RELIEF

Read 2 Corinthians 1:3-7.

"Just as the sufferings of Christ flow over into our lives, so also through Christ our comfort overflows" (v. 5).

Tommy Hodson was in such pain that he expected to sit out the rest of the game. He wound up leading the Tigers to a victory.

Hodson is the only Tiger to be named first-team All-SEC four times. He was the first quarterback in SEC history to surpass 8,000 career passing yards. He led the Tigers to two SEC titles, as a freshman in 1986 and as a junior in 1988.

When LSU met Kentucky the fifth game of his freshman season, Hodson was still trying to prove himself. "I hadn't yet solidified myself as a starter. I really needed to do something to fortify my starting role," he said. It didn't look as though he would get the chance this day when he threw a pass early in the game, was hit by a blitzing Wildcat, and bit right through his tongue.

A local dentist led Hodson to the dressing room. "I was kind of out of it, kind of incoherent," Hodson said. The dentist's report wasn't encouraging: "You bit all the way through it." The bite was so deep that he had to put three stitches on the top and two on the bottom to get Hodson's tongue back together.

"I thought I was going to sit out the rest of the game," Hodson said. But when he returned to the sideline, Kentucky led 7-0 and Coach Bill Arnsparger ordered him back into the game. "I said 'OK.' I just went in there and started throwing the ball around and

TIGERS

didn't care about much. I don't think my mind was right."

There was nothing wrong with his arm, though. Hodson completed 16 of 24 passes for 255 yards with two touchdowns and no interceptions. LSU won 25-16.

Hodson's tongue eventually healed. "The only thing I have is a little scar beneath my chin," he said. He admitted that the story and the legend grew over the years, but he did go out and play after not just biting his tongue, but biting through it.

Since you live on Earth and not in Heaven, you are forced to play with pain. Whether it's a car wreck that left you shattered, the end of a relationship that left you battered, or a loved one's death that left you tattered -- pain finds you and challenges you to keep going.

While God's word teaches that you will reap what you sow, life also teaches that pain and hardship are not necessarily the result of personal failure. Pain in fact can be one of the tools God uses to mold your character and change your life.

What are you to do when you are hit full-speed by the awful pain that seems to choke the very will to live out of you? Where is your consolation, your comfort, and your help?

In almighty God, whose love will never fail. When life knocks you to your knees, you're closer to God than ever before.

People just thought it was the biggest thing, that I bit my tongue and played.

-- *Tommy Hodson*

**When life hits you with pain, you can always
turn to God for comfort, consolation, and hope.**

THE END

Read Revelation 22:1-17.

"I am the Alpha and the Omega, the First and the Last, the Beginning and the End" (v. 13).

After more than 125 years and almost one hundred games, it ended.

In September 2009, LSU and Tulane announced the end of their football series. They had previously signed a ten-year contract in 2005 in an attempt to resuscitate the series that had been dormant since the 1996 game, but by joint agreement the 2009 game was the finale.

Thus ended one of the South's oldest rivalries. LSU's first-ever football game was against Tulane on Nov. 25, 1883. The Olive and Blue won that contest quite handily, as expected. Good sportsmanship prevailed, the *Daily Picayune* reporting, "The game was without the smallest exhibition of ill temper and the Baton Rouge boys took their defeat good-humoredly."

That didn't last long as the game "quickly turned into internecine warfare -- bloodless but blood-broiling." Neither did the competitive nature of the rivalry. Except for a brief period of Green Wave glory between 1920 and 1940 -- when Tulane won twelve of the twenty games -- LSU thoroughly dominated what increasingly became a one-sided rivalry. The decision in 2009 was a concession that the schools just didn't fit into each other's plans anymore.

TIGERS

Tulane was a force to be reckoned with in the late 1940s. All that changed, though, in 1949, when LSU upset the Green Wave 21-0 on a day when LSU guard Charles Cusimano admitted, "Tulane's third team was better than our first team." But LSU won and so has it been practically ever since.

With LSU's win in 2009, the final series record stood at 69-22-7, reflecting a dominance that long ago took the heat out of the rivalry. For now and for the foreseeable future, it has ended.

The LSU-Tulane series is just another example of one of life's basic truths: Everything ends. Even the stars have a life cycle, though admittedly it's rather lengthy. Erosion eventually will wear a boulder to a pebble. Life itself is temporary; all living things have a beginning and an end.

Within the framework of our individual lifetimes, we meet endings. Loved ones, friends, and pets die; relationships fracture; jobs dry up; our health, clothes, lawn mowers, TV sets – they all wear out. Even this world as we know it will end.

But one of the greatest ironies of God's gift of life is that not even death is immune from the great truth of creation that all things must end. That's because through Jesus' life, death, and resurrection, God himself acted to end any power death once had over life. In other words, because of Jesus, the end of life has ended. Eternity is ours for the claiming.

Things change. So no hard feelings.
-- Tulane AD Rick Dickson on the end of the LSU-Tulane football series

Everything ends; thanks to Jesus Christ,
so does death.

NOTES
(by Devotion Day Number)

1   he was surprised by . . . both scholarship and athletics.: Marty Mule, *Eye of the Tiger* (Atlanta: Longstreet Press, 1993), p. 1.

1   in the fall of 1893, . . . nailed cleats on leather shoes.: Mule, *Eye of the Tiger*, p. 2.

1   The daily scrimmages began . . . excitement around town,: Dan Hardesty, *The Louisiana Tigers* (Huntsville, AL: The Strode Publishers, 1975), p. 15.

1   The *Baton Rouge Daily* . . . to New Orleans: Hardesty, p. 15.

1   ticket prices for the game . . . cheer lustily for the cadets.": Hardesty, p. 16.

1   The afternoon was cold . . . selecting Professor Coates.: Hardesty, p. 18.

1   It struck me we ought to have that sort of thing.: Mule, *Eye of the Tiger*, p. 1.

2   After starting 41 of the . . . season's final sixteen games.: Randy Rosetta, "Ochinko Delivers After Move to Clean-Up," *The Advocate*, June 25, 2009, http://www.2theadvocate.com/sports/lsu/49056876.html, June 25, 2009.

2   a spot Ochinko had not occupied since April 22.: Rosetta, "Ochinko Delivers."

2   He moved Ochinko into . . . the College World Series.: Rosetta, "Ochinko Delivers."

2   He drilled the first pitch he saw: Rosetta, "Ochinko Delivers."

2   He told me he wasn't . . . and he didn't.: Rosetta, "Ochinko Delivers."

3   the Wildcat head coach . . . score on the screen:: Marty Mule, *Game of My Life* (Champaign, IL: Sports Publishing L.L.C., 2006), p. 91.

3   with all the arm strength . . . to be a Kentucky player.: Mule, *Game of My Life*, p. 93.

3   As "Dash-right-93 . . . I couldn't believe it.": Mule, *Game of My Life*, p. 96.

3   It was just a freak, unbelievable thing.: Mule, *Game of My Life*, p. 91.

4   He held for extra points . . . was tempted to transfer,: Austin Murphy, "The 2007 BCS Championship," *Sports Illustrated Presents LSU Tigers: 2007 National Champions*, Jan. 16, 2008, p. 39.

4   his parents faithfully drove . . . for all the games: Murphy, p. 44.

4   "This isn't how I would have . . . it's so, so sweet.": Murphy, p. 44.

4   I wouldn't give up . . . starting anywhere else.: Murphy, p. 44.

5   Holt was an "up-and-coming LSU receiver": Mule, *Game of My Life*, pp. 62-63.

5   Until 1985, there was . . . that short south end zone.: Mule, *Game of My Life*, p. 62.

5   During spring training in 1985, went their separate ways.: Mule, *Game of My Life*, p. 63.

6   Five times a day. . . . when she was at LSU.: Kelli Anderson, "Beware of Tigers," *Sports Illustrated*, March 24, 2008, http://sportsillustrated.cnn.com/vault/article/magazine/MAG1127561/index.htm, Nov. 1, 2009.

6   Coach Van Chancellor once . . . aren't supposed to see.": Anderson, "Beware of Tigers."

7   a 40-minute delay: "Game 1," *Tiger Terrific!* (Chicago: Triumph Books, 2004), p. 28.

7   "caught a bit of the Louisiana lightning in a bottle,": "Game 1," p. 28.

TIGERS

7	"It was raining pretty hard . . . got more comfortable.": "Game 1," p. 28.
8	"Coach Mac was really . . . and class that he had.": Lee Feinswog, *Tales from the LSU Sidelines* (Champaign, IL: Sports Publishing L.L.C., 2002), p. 176.
8	"Coach Mac gave everything . . . more than himself.": Feinswog, p. 177.
8	"I would like to be . . . live a little better.": Feinswog, p. 177.
8	"We lost a fine man . . . never be forgotten.": Feinswog, p. 178.
8	I want my family . . . while we were together.: Feinswog, p. 177.
9	"a perennial sophomore when . . . band down the field.: Mule, *Eye of the Tiger*, p. 46.
9	He stormed into the dressing . . . "That's a bargain,": Mule, *Eye of the Tiger*, p. 50.
9	He quit. . . . he didn't want to leave.": Mule, *Eye of the Tiger*, p. 50.
10	"the longest one-mile move in program history.": David Helman, "Softball: Current, Former Tigers Excited About Stadium Advancements," *Daily Reveille*, Feb. 16, 2009, http://www.lsureveille.com/softball-current-former-tigers-excited-about-stadium-advance, Oct. 29, 2009.
10	Coach Yvette Girouard had begun . . . the field I started on,": Helman.
10	old Tiger Park was not . . . worth well more than that.": Matt Deville, "Girouard, LSU Ready to Take the Field at New Tiger Park," *TigerRag.com*, Feb. 11, 2009, http://www.tigerrag.com/?p=6661, Oct. 29, 1009.
10	Tiger Park is by far . . . blessed to be playing here.: "Know Your Softball Tigers -- Anissa Young and Kirsten Shortridge," *LSUsports.net*, Feb. 2, 2009, http://www.lsusports.net/ViewArticle.dbml, Oct. 29, 2009.
11	Entering Louisiana. Set your watches back four seconds.": Mule, *Game of My Life*, p. 119.
11	"Year of the Miracle," Hardesty, p. 289.
11	"engineered the best pressure drive in Tiger Stadium history." Hardesty, p. 290.
11	"Bert, this is what you came to LSU for.": Mule, *Game of My Life*, p. 119.
11	"You know what [Jones] . . . He winked at me.": Mule, *Eye of the Tiger*, p. 173.
11	When you're standing back there . . . that's pressure.: Hardesty, p. 291.
12	Coach Dale Brown called the best captain he ever had: Bruce Hunter and Joe Planas, *Fighting Tigers Basketball* (Chicago: Bonus Books, Inc. 1991), p. 40.
12	"didn't figure into LSU's plans . . . into his plans either.: Hunter and Planas, p. 41.
12	"he was suddenly in over his head talent-wise.": Hunter and Planas, p. 40.
12	But he wanted to play, . . . made a wise move.": Hunter and Planas, p. 41.
12	LSU needed help at . . . he became a starter,: Hunter and Planas, p. 41.
13	"Everybody counted us out after we lost to Arkansas,": Randy Rosetta, "Tigers Ecstatic about Chance to Play for Title," *The Advocate*, Dec. 3, 2007, http://docs.newsbank.com/s/InfoWeb/aggdocs/NewsBank, Jan. 20, 2010.
13	On the charter flight . . . the West Virginia game,": Rosetta, "Tigers Ecstatic."
13	"Then he told us . . . in the fourth quarter.": Rosetta, "Tigers Ecstatic."
13	So when the Tigers . . . at 7:21 p.m.,: Rosetta, "Tigers Ecstatic"
13	It seemed like it . . . who was going to play.: Rosetta, "Tigers

Ecstatic."

14   "a masterful game plan" that was executed "almost flawlessly": Mule, *Game of My Life*, p. 236.

14   DiNardo decided to "smack . . . a new belly play.": Mule, *Game of My Life*, p. 237.

14   the Tigers kept the starters . . . line and linebacker reserves.: Mule, Game of My Life, p. 237.

14   We won that game . . . and we were ready.": Mule, *Game of My Life*, p. 237.

15   the only player named . . . Team of the Century.: Mule, *Eye of the Tiger*, p. 52.

15   LSU was backed up to . . . down the left sideline.: Hardesty, p. 116.

15   When you run trick plays . . . folks question your sanity.: Jim & Julie S. Bettinger, *The Book of Bowden* (Nashville: TowleHouse Publishing, 2001), p. 32.

16   "a streak that stands . . . collegiate athletics to this day.: "Dominance on the Track," *2010 LSU Track & Field Media Guide*, p. 10, LSUsports.net, Feb. 10, 2010.

16   On the last day of . . . the fifth-place Sun Devils.: Sheldon Mickles, "Right on Track," *The Advocate*, June 15, 2008, http://docs.newsbank.com/s/InfoWeb/aggdocs/NewsBank, Jan. 21, 2010.

17   A rule change in 1958 . . . which had questionable depth.: Mule, *Eye of the Tiger*, p. 134.

17   Coach Paul Dietzel divided . . . and third-string backs.: Mule, *Eye of the Tiger*, p. 135.

17   "It took guts,": Mule, *Eye of the Tiger*, p. 136.

17   When Life magazine . . . focused on the Bandits.: Mule, *Eye of the Tiger*, p. 138.

17   Dietzel got the idea . . . vicious people on earth.": Mule, Eye of the Tiger, p. 136.

17   The greatest thrill . . . associated with the Bandits.: Mule, *Eye of the Tiger*, p. 138.

18   she had recently undergone root canal surgery.: "1976-77: The Only Lady Tigers to Reach the National Championship Game of a Post-Season Tournament," *2006-07 LSU Women's Basketball Media Guide*, p. 147, http://www.lsusports.net/ViewArticle.dbml, Nov. 2, 2009.

19   in the dressing room . . . didn't say a word.": Mule, *Game of My Life*, p. 4.

19   Again, McClendon had to . . would get better: Mule, *Game of My Life*, p. 4.

19   Not many backs can . . . ready to do it again.: Mule, *Game of My Life*, p. 6.

20   "It was killing me," . . . putting my shoes on.": Feinswog, p. 11.

20   he had to tell people . . . and two bulging discs.: Feinswog, p. 10.

20   At the last scrimmage of . . . But it never did.": Feinswog, p. 12.

20   The last two years . . . I thank God for that.: Feinswog, p. 12.

21   In 1986, LSU coach . . . tour of coaching clinics.: Curry Kirkpatrick, "Shack Attack," *Sports Illustrated*, Jan. 21, 1991, http://sportsillustrated.cnn.com/vault/article/magazine/MAG1118770/index.htm, Dec. 1, 2009.

21   On a U.S. Army base in West Germany,: Hunter and Planas, p. 25.

21   Brown entertained a crowd . . . improving his jumping ability.: Hunter and Planas, p. 26.

21   the young man's 6'6" . . . "Uh, your dad around?": Kirkpatrick.

21   Brown told O'Neal he was . . . letters from Coach Brown.": Hunter and

Planas, p. 26.

22   "seemed about half empty.": Carl Dubois, "LSU Opener Anything But Normal," *The Advocate*, Aug. 31, 2008, http://docs.newsbank.com/s/InfoWeb/aggdocs/Newsbank, Jan. 21, 2010.

22   The student section was . . . and the national anthem.: Dubois, "LSU Opener."

22   a pregame intonation from . . . morning in Tiger Stadium.": Dubois, "LSU Opener."

22   "It's the earliest kickoff . . . "I'm not a morning person.": Carl Dubois, "Game Too Early for Some," *The Advocate*, Aug. 31, 2008, http://docs.newsbank.com/s/InfoWeb/aggdocs/NewsBank, Jan. 21, 2010.

22   State officials had declared . . . or none at all.: Dubois, "LSU Opener."

22   folks fled for . . . and/or the shade.: Dubois, "LSU Opener."

23   In the summer of 1931, . . . Foley's home in Oklahoma,: Mule, *Eye of the Tiger*, p. 47.

23   found him on vacation . . . for LSU in the fall.: Mule, *Eye of the Tiger*, p. 48.

23   Since he was a junior- . . . debut against Spring Hill.: Mule, *Eye of the Tiger*, p. 49.

23   Long and head coach Russ Cohen . . . Heard told him the news.: Mule, *Eye of the Tiger*, p. 49.

23   No one knows when . . . blink of an eye.: Bettinger, p. 21.

24   "That's No. 1 because . . . in the Skip Bertman era.: Glenn Guilbeau, "Top 10 Games of Bertman Era," *The Advocate*, May 13, 2001. http://docs.newsbank.com/s/InfoWeb/aggdocs/NewsBank, Jan. 19, 2010.

24   No. 2 on the list . . . the repeat national title.: Guilbeau, "Top 10 Games."

25   Baton Rouge wins without winning.": Hardesty, p. 24.

25   "it offered six courses . . . and medical attendance.": Hardesety, p. 25.

25   Tulane led 2-0 on . . . was an illegal player.: Hardesty, p. 24

25   LSU's position was that . . . to sign that affidavit.: Hardesty, p. 25.

25   The referee, a Lt. Wall, . . . the interruption of the sport.": Hardesty, p. 24.

25   Wall fixed the final . . . at 6-0.: Hardesty, p. 25.

25   LSU can't have a losing . . . associated with a loser.: *SEC Sports Quotes*, Ed. Chris Warner (Baton Rouge: CEW Enterprises, 2002), p. 155.

26   "Frustrating" and "embarrassing": Scott Rabalais, "LSU Comeback Beyond Words," *The Advocate*, March 21, 2003, http://docs.newsbank.com/s/InfoWeb/aggdocs/NewsBank, Jan 19, 2010.

26   "looked bad doing it . . . No. 1 seed to fall.: Rabalais, "LSU Comeback."

26   Coach Sue Gunter blistered her team at halftime: Rabalais, "LSU Comeback."

26   "a volcanic eruption . . . to that point.": Rabalais, "LSU Comeback."

26   Gunter admitted that . . . in such a big game.: Rabalais, "LSU Comeback."

27   The school changed the rules . . . such a part of it.": Mule, *Game of My Life*, p. 135.

27   "That was a disappointment," . . . think He blessed me.": Mule, *Game of My Life*, p. 135.

27   "as spectacular a performance . . . turned in around here.: Mule, *Game of My Life*, p. 134.

27   "dazzling dashes": Mule, *Game of My Life*, p. 134.

27   For Todd, playing for LSU . . . who had gone before him.:

Mule, *Game of My Life*, p. 137.

28   On the morning of the game, . . . talking to anyone else.": Cory McCartney, "One Title Down, One More to Go," *Sports Illustrated Presents LSU Tigers: 2007 National Champions*, Jan. 16, 2008, p. 35.

28   Their formation had Zenon 'salivating' because he knew what was coming.: McCartney, "One Title Down," p. 35.

28   I knew exactly what they were going to run.: McCartney. "One Title Down," p. 35.

29   "dedicated, possessed, and obsessed," . . . and make a million dollars.": "Shoot out the Moon," *LSU Campus: LSU Highlights Spring 2005*, http://www.lsu.edu/highlights/051/maravich.html, Oct. 5, 2009.

29   he was searching for . . . no meaning at all.": Shoot out the Moon."

29   his message that through . . . basketball player he had been.: "Shoot out the Moon."

29   If you focus on . . . fleeting moment in life.: "Shoot out the Moon."

30   with new and stronger . . . for a Halloween game.": Hardesty, p. 208.

30   worn and beaten for the first time in 18 games.": Mule, *Eye of the Tiger*, p. 57.

30   "We had a rule . . . to bring it back.": Mule, *Eye of the Tiger*, p. 57.

30   "and started an incredible, absolutely unbelievable run to glory.": Hardesty, p. 211.

30   He was hit almost right . . . would-be tackler at midfield": Mule, *Eye of the Tiger*, p. 57.

30   "a white-shirted ghost wearing jersey number 20.: Hardesty, p. 208.

30   That was the greatest run I ever saw in football.: Mule, *Eye of the Tiger*, p. 58.

31   "game is not merely seen. It is HEARD.": John Logue quoted in *SEC Sports Quotes*, Ed. Chris Warner, p. 160.

31   "The Golden Band from . . . still uses the sousaphones.: Frank B. Wickes, "LSU Band History," *LSU Department of Bands*, http://www.bands.lsu.edu/band_history/index.php, Sept. 23, 2009.

32   On Dec. 16, 2007, . . . his leukemia in remission.: Randy Rosetta, "Source of Strength," *The Advocate*, Dec. 25, 2009, http://docs.newsbank.com/s/InfoWeb/aggdocs/NewsBank, Jan. 21, 2010.

32   Some people see us . . . are the real heroes.: Rosetta, "Source of Strength."

33   Davis walked off the court . . . since the seventh grade.: Randy Rosetta, "Big Makeover," *The Advocate*, July 30, 2006, http://docs.newsbank.com/s/InfoWeb/aggdocs/NewsBank, Jan. 20, 2010.

33   By the time we got . . . where it needs to be.: Rosetta, "Big Makeover."

34   "bouncing around the LSU . . . important to get it back.": Scott Rabalais, "LSU's Robinson Enjoys Practice," *The Advocate*, March 26, 2002, http://docs.newsbank.com/s/InfoWeb/aggdocs/NewsBank, Jan. 19, 2010.

34   Shortly before fall practice . . . I'm happy to go.": Rabalais, "LSU's Robinson."

35   LSU's cadets couldn't afford . . . hop the Sunday freight.: Hardesty, p. 52.

35   The cadets had placed . . . on a passenger train.: Hardesty, p. 52.

35   A traffic survey in . . . their way into town.: Hardesty, p. 56.

36   The Tigers got inside . . . his yard at home.: Mule, *Game of My Life*, p. 178.

36   "I needed it," . . . to catch my breath.": Mule, *Game of My Life*, p. 178.

36   The Lord taught me . . . were the sportswriters.: Chris Warner, p. 135.

37   When he was ten, his . . . playing the game again,: Randy Rosetta, "Giving Back," *The Advocate*, July 18, 2008, http://docs.newsbank.com/s/InfoWeb/ aggdocs/NewsBank, Jan. 21, 2010.

37   he never had the chance . . . "Couldn't afford it,": Tim MacMahon, "Brandon Bass' Camp Is Just the Beginning," *Dallas Mavericks Blog*, June 21, 2008, http://mavsblog.dallasnews.com/archives/2008/06, Feb. 5, 2010.

37   he "didn't have any inspiration, . . . give something back.": Rosetta, "Giving Back."

38   Only after the public address . . . the riotous LSU stands.: Bernell Ballard, "Tigers Stun Ole Miss, Orange Bowl Brass," *Greatest Moments in LSU Football History*, Francis J. Fitzgerald, ed. (Champaign, IL: Sports Publishing L.L.C., 2002), p. 89.

38   "the most important victory . . . I have ever seen.": Ballard, p. 89.

38   [The LSU win] assures the . . . New Year's but ever.: Ballard, p. 89.

39   He is credited with creating the power forward position: "Bob Pettit," *Wikipedia, the free encyclopedia*, http://en.wikipedia.org/wiki/Bob_Pettit, Nov. 30, 2009.

39   "I had never played . . . in cars for everyone.: Hunter and Planas, p. 70.

39   After he was cut . . . then practiced some more: Hunter and Planas, p. 70.

39   once declaring that his . . . pushed him to improve.: Hunter and Planas, p. 69.

39   If things come naturally, . . . short of your potential.: Hunter and Planas, p. 69.

40   Expectations were that . . . Thanksgiving Day 1924: Hardesty, p. 60.

40   The concrete stands weren't . . . stadium was roped off.: Hardesty, p. 62.

40   Adequate roads for cars . . . the bulk of the crowd.: Hardestry, pp. 62-63.

40   The new facility didn't have . . . the rest of the way.: Hardesty, p. 64.

40   There are very few stadiums . . . that advantage in Tiger Stadium.: "Tiger Stadium," *2009 LSU Football Media Guide*, p. 185, http://www.lsusports.net/ ViewArticle.dmbl, Sept. 23, 2009.

41   Sugar bowl officials started . . . Tigers were capable of.: Hardesty, p. 164.

41   "the group sitting in . . . agreed to the bowl game.: Hardesty, p. 165.

41   We've made an agreement and we'll live up to it.": Hardesty, p. 165.

42   Throughout the tournament, the . . . an opponent until that day.: Brian Hendrickson, "LSU Fans Prove to Be a Class Act in Regionals," *Wilmington Star-News*, June 2, 2003, reprinted in *The Advocate*, June 22, 2003, http:// docs.newsbank.com/s/InfoWeb/aggdocs/NewsBank.

42   "I've never seen anything like this.": Hendrickson.

43   His typical daily diet . . . horse meat and cereal.: Feinswong, p. 102.

43   arrangements were made to . . . the students relented.: Feinswong, p. 103.

43   I am on as close . . . curl up and die.: Feinswong, p. 103.

44   Some board members thought . . . granted Dietzel's request.: Hardesty, p. 228.

44   Athletic Director Jim Corbett immediately . . . to consider and contact them.: Hardesty, p. 229.

44   That same day, McClendon, . . . his for the taking.: Hardesty, p. 231.

44   calling Kentucky and . . . to stay at LSU.: Hardesty, pp. 231-32.

44   the only two jobs I . . . It was unreal.: Hardesty, p. 232.

45   "in a poorly lighted hall . . . win over Dixon Academy.:

Hunter and Planas, p. 115.

45 "This victory was quite . . . delighted" with the win.: Hunter and Planas, p. 116.

45 "that same season, the LSU coeds . . . "only defeated once.": Hunter and Planas, p. 115.

45 Annie Boyd, for whom . . . and Ida Howell.: Hunter and Planas, pp. 115-16.

45 Life is an adventure. . . . going to happen next.: Bettinger, p. 74.

46 he didn't look like much. . . . "the runt of the litter.": Mule, *Game of My Life*, p. 218.

46 His high school coach said, . . . to be an All-American,": Mule, *Game of My Life*, p. 219.

46 "there were lots of bigger . . . for just a little longer.": Mule, *Game of My Life*, p. 219.

47 both years delayed the . . . the mail was fumigated.: Hardesty, p. 26.

47 "had been so occasioned . . . time to field practice.": Hardesty, p. 27.

48 If you study this game . . . played a perfect game.: Hardesty, p. 253.

48 Thanks largely to the persuasive . . . had blown a fuse.": Hardesty, p. 250.

48 "The Tigers were hopelessly . . . had them superbly prepared." Hardesty, p. 250.

48 We didn't make a mistake. . . . this kind of football.: Hardesty, p. 253.

49 You have ten guys . . . who can beat me?": Hunter and Planas, p. 89.

49 "with a dollar in . . . engendered by his size:: Hunter and Planas, p. 84.

49 "basketball is the silliest game in the world": Hunter and Planas, p. 89.

49 "a super showman," . . . including dance on it." Hunter and Planas, p. 83.

49 "he was confident he . . . to let it go.": Hunter and Planas, p. 84.

49 they double- and triple-teamed him: Hunter and Planas, p. 84.

49 He spent the night . . . with perfect passes,: Hunter and Planas, p. 84.

49 I think God made it simple. Just accept Him and believe.: Bettinger, p. 47.

50 "Initially, I didn't . . . the upper layers of the earth.: Kristine Calongne, "After 15 years, LSU-Auburn Game Still an Earthshaking Experience," *LSU Campus: LSU Highlights Winter 2003*, http://www.lsu.edu/highlights/ 033/football.html, Sept. 24, 2009.

50 Both Hodson and Fuller . . . they had ever played.: Calongne.

51 The Tigers made their . . . to hit the ground.": Hardesty, p. 138.

51 Few of the players . . . pilot in World War II.: Hardesty, pp. 138-39.

51 He said he might start . . . supposed to be played.: Hardesty, p. 139.

52 "nearly 4 1/2 hours of unspeakable drama.": Scott Rabalais, "LSU Stays Alive with High Drama," *The Advocate*, May 21, 2000, http://docs.news-bank.com/s/InfoWeb/aggdocs/NewsBank, Jan 19, 2010.

52 the home-plate umpire . . . "As long as it takes.": Rabalais, "LSU Stays."

52 "Our intensity never failed," . . . made we never faltered.": Rabalais, LSU Stays."

52 Both teams refused . . . of sweat and blood.: Rabalais, "LSU Stays."

53 Everybody except LSU and . . . better than anyone we have.": Mule, *Eye of the Tiger*, p. 195.

53 he "seemed to glide . . . the laws of physics.": Mule, *Eye of the Tiger*, p. 195.

53 "People were wondering if . . . tackle on him yet.": Mule, *Eye of the Tiger*, p. 197.

53 "the size of most male waists.": Mule, *Eye of the Tiger*, p. 196.

53 legs sturdy as pillars.: Mule, *Eye of the Tiger*, p. 197.

53 [Dalton Hilliard's doctor . . . in medical school.: Mule, *Eye of the Tiger*, p. 197.

54 After working out with him, . . . he was so bad.: Mule, *Game of My Life*, p. 64.

54 Wendell Davis was not . . . not overly impressed,": Mule, *Game of My Life*, p. 64.

54 He had an incredibly . . . stick to those hands.: Mule, *Game of My Life*, p. 64.

54 When Hodson got the . . . to throw to: Davis.": Mule, *Game of My Life*, p. 66.

54 My father is the person . . . duties at home.: Mule, *Game of My Life*, p. 64.

55 "I have played a square . . . ashamed of my record.": Hardesty, p. 49.

55 Fans and players alike . . . grinding season began.: Hardesty, p. 49.

55 So athletic officials began . . . they went nowhere.: Hardesty, pp. 49-50.

55 lit out for Cuba . . . finish the season as head coach.: Hardesty, p. 50.

55 Would it not be worth . . . could be made successful?: Hardesty, p. 51.

55 "ambivalent, vacillating, impulsive, unsubmissive.": John MacArthur, *Twelve Ordinary Men* (Nashville: W Publishing Group, 2002), p. 39.

55 "the greatest preacher . . . birth of the church.": MacArthur, p. 39.

55 Would it not be worth . . . could be made successful?: Hardesty, p. 51.

56 Some players were surprised by . . . led his team in prayer.: Bruce Hunter, *Don't Count Me Out* (Chicago: Bonus Books, Inc., 1989), p. 6.

56 At that time in his life, . . . at home in his study.": Hunter, p. 9.

56 the response was "almost automatic.": Hunter, p. 8.

56 Brown "hadn't put much . . . his nickname, "Preacher Man,": Hunter, p. 6.

56 had appointed a spiritual . . . sermon before each game.: Hunter, p. 6.

56 His wife, Vonnie, had become . . . to turn to Christ.: Hunter, p. 8.

56 the way he coached games, . . . reached out to others.: Hunter, p. 9.

56 When everyone else is down . . . always lifting us up.: Hunter, p. 8.

57 "Contemporary football players don't . . . married, hard-nosed runner.": Andrew Lawrence, "Golden Oldie," *Sports Illustrated Presents LSU Tigers: 2007 National Champions*, Jan. 16, 2008, p. 55.

57 Hester was most often . . . once the entire season.: Lawrence, p. 56.

57 who was named for the lead character in *Big Jake*,: Lawrence, p. 57.

57 "the consummate throwback player,": Lawrence, p. 56.

57 "I guess I am . . . an old-school player.": Lawrence, p. 56.

57 Against Tennessee in 2006, . . . back for Air Force?": Lawrence, p. 57.

57 I guess I was born a little too late.: Lawrence, p. 56.

58 His first day on campus . . . can't take any plays off.": Randy Rosetta, "Happy to Be There," *The Advocate*, Sept. 10, 2008, http://docs.newsbank.com/s/InfoWeb/aggdocs/NewsBank, Jan. 21, 2010.

58 I love being an . . . was meant to be.: Rosetta, "Happy to Be There."

59 "Everything we did at LSU . . . timed to perfection.": Feinswog, p. 58.

59 the schedule for game day . . . Coach Dietzel's meetings,": Feinswog, p. 59.

59 To this day, I . . . on Central Dietzel Time.: Feinswog, p. 59.

60 Cresse raised his right arm . . . as far as he could.: Glenn Guilbeau, "Amazing: Dream Comes True as LSU Wins Thriller for Fifth National Title," *The Advocate*, June 18, 2000, http://docs.newsbank.com/s/InfoWeb/aggdocs/NewsBank, Jan. 19, 2010.

60 Skip Bertman eschewed the dogpile . . . may be the best

ever.": Sam King, "Bertman Believes this One May Be Best Yet," *The Advocate*, June 18, 2000, http://docs.newsbank.com/s/InfoWeb/aggdocs/ NewsBank, Jan. 19, 2010.

60   This is the first time I'm tearless for more than a minute.: Guilbeau, "Amazing."

61   "to moon an opponent . . . make the Hall of Fame.": Mule, *Eye of the Tiger*, p. 103.

61   he asked LSU publicist . . . T-formation passer and quarterback.": Mule, *Eye of the Tiger*, pp. 105-06.

61   The Rebels were ahead . . . to be Tittle's belt buckle.": Mule, *Eye of the Tiger*, p. 103.

61   "I was racing down the field . . . down if he hadn't.: Mule, *Eye of the Tiger*, p. 104.

61   I'm not sure if I could have scored or not.: Mule, *Eye of the Tiger*, p. 104.

62   "On paper, they appeared to be almost unbeatable,": *Tiger Terrific*, p. 6.

62   "records would fall, . . . become national champions.": *Tiger Terrific*, p. 6.

62   The Sooners were so confident . . . how we want to play.": *Tiger Terrific*, p. 10.

62   Early in the season, . . . college teams of all time.: *Tiger Terrific*, p. 6.

63   SEC teams had no experience . . . the three-headed calf.": Kent Lowe, Sr., "Look Back: 20 Years after LSU, Loyola Marymount," *LSUsports.net*, Feb. 3, 2010, http://www.lsusports.net/ViewArticle.dbml, Feb. 3, 2010.

63   The scoring was so fast . . . the motor burned up.: Lowe.

63   Crazy like a fox.: Lowe.

64   The Tigers would have more . . . he never considered it.: Randy Rosetta, "Miles Never Considered Conceding TD to State," *The Advocate*, Sept. 28, 2009, http://docs.newsbank.com/s/InfoWeb/aggdocs/NewsBank, Jan. 21, 2010.

64   after instructing the linebackers to watch the run.: Randy Rosetta, "Taking a Stand," *The Advocate*, Sept. 27, 2009, http://docs.newsbank.com/s/InfoWeb/ aggdocs/NewsBank, Jan. 21, 2010.

64   linebacker Kelvin Sheppard hit . . . by knocking him backward.: Rosetta, "Taking a Stand."

64   It's amazing. Some of . . . to be a Christian man.: Bettinger, p. 121.

65   he often visited practices . . . senators of the whole team.: Mule, *Eye of the Tiger*, p. 43.

65   Mickal refused to report . . . Mickal's amateur standing.: Mule, *Eye of the Tiger*, p. 44.

65   Maybe they ought to try making something of their senators.: Mule: *Eye of the Tiger*, p. 44.

66   "a fortnight of the chaos . . . aftermath of Hurricane Katrina.": Kelli Anderson, "Home Is Where the Heart Is," *Sports Illustrated*, Sept. 19, 2005, http:// vault.sportsillustrated.cnn.com/vault/article/magazine/MAG1106374/ index.htm, July 10, 2009.

66   "We wanted to win for . . . displaced relatives and friends.: Anderson, "Home Is Where the Heart Is."

66   They helped pay the . . . grits to the breakfast menu.: Anderson, "Home Is Where the Heart Is."

66   "We were not going to give up,": Anderson, "Home Is Where the Heart Is."

67   "It was the very sort . . . baseball in the backyard." "Warren Morris." *TheGoal.com*. http://www.ghegoal.com/players/baseball/morris_warren/ morris_warren.html, Feb. 6, 2010.

67   "the lowest point in my . . . had a broken bone.: "Warren Morris."

68   Chase was a junior in . . . never going to happen.": Randy Rosetta, "Playing with Pain," *The Advocate*, Aug. 20, 2006, http://docs.newsbank.com/s/ InfoWeb/aggdocs/Newsbank., Jan. 20, 2010.

68   Over his heart, he had . . . never too far away.": Rosetta, "Playing with Pain."

68   Whenever I walk out . . . I'm thinking about him.: Rosetta, "Playing with Pain."

69   In 1896, "Drum," the pet . . . sewn on their jackets.: Mule, *Eye of the Tiger*, p. 5.

69   As the 1896 season . . . known as the Tigers.: Mule, *Eye of the Tige*r, p. 7.

69   The reference was probably . . . from Yankee body parts.: Mule, *Eye of the Tiger*, p. 6

69   The first live cat . . . during the 1920s and '30s.: Feinswog, p. 95.

69   until Mike Chambers, a football . . . Originally named Sheik,: Feinswog, p. 98.

69   the Tiger's name was changed . . . of the whole idea.: Feinswog, p. 99.

69   We wanted a mascot that could stand up and roar.: Feinswog, p. 98.

70   an unlikely Moses, . . . arm and wiggly feet.": Jimmy Hyams, "Risher & Tigers Upset Alabama, 20-10," *The Greatest Moments in LSU Football History*, Francis J. Fitzgerald, ed. (Champaign, IL: Sports Publishing L.L.C., 2002), 112.

70   "without a doubt, . . . had as a coach,": Hyams, p. 113.

70   "You can't understand . . . 11 years in a row.": Hyams, pp. 113-14.

70   "the best beating we've had since the 1960's.": Hyams, p. 114.

70   This end twelve years . . . a fan and player.: Hyams, p. 113.

71   Harry Rabenhorst was "a great model . . . productive, responsible life.": Hunter and Planas, p. 108.

71   "was the most pure . . . want to meet in life,": Hunter and Planas, pp. 103-04.

71   Rabenhorst was "a man of . . . play by the rules.: Hunter and Planas, p. 108.

71   He once left a baseball . . . after the departing bus.: Hunter and Planas, p. 108.

71   I have never known . . . than Coach Raby.: Hunter and Planas, p. 108.

72   Ladies and gentlemen, . . . Fighting Tigers of LSU.": "Saturday Night in Death Valley," *2009 LSU Football Media Guide*, p. 34, http://www.lsusports. net/ViewArticle.dmbl, Oct. 5, 2009.

72   The idea was the brainchild . . . to see the Tigers play.: "LSU Football Traditions A to Z," *2009 LSU Football Media Guide*, p. 63, http://www.lsu sports.net/ViewArticle.dmbl, Oct. 5, 2009.

72   "a nocturnal spectacle . . . aspect delightfully theatrical.": Hardesty, p. 81.

72   Reserved sideline seats were . . . for one thin dime.: Hardesty, p. 82.

72   "the freakiest, funkiest . . . in all of college football.": Matt Hayes, *Sporting News Today*, quoted in "Saturday Night in Death Valley," p. 34.

72   Dracula and LSU football . . . the sun goes down.: "Tiger Stadium," p. 185.

73   After the 2007 national . . . players I've ever seen.": Murphy, p. 41.

73   He still has a slight bow to his legs,: Cory McCartney, "A Tiger Unchained," *Sports Illustrated Presents LSU Tigers: 2007 National Champions*,
Jan. 16, 2008, p. 49.

73   fueled Dorsey's unrelenting drive.: McCartney, "A Tiger Unchained,"
p. 48.

73   In 1988, 3-year-old . . . while his friends played.: McCartney, "A Tiger
Unchained," p. 47.

73   "I was on the porch, just watching everybody,": Murphy, p. 40.

73   He took a football . . . dreamed of playing.: John K. Davis, "Glenn Dorsey:
Key to LSU Defense," *suite101.com*, Jan. 5, 2008, http://college-football.
suite101.com/article.com/glenn_dorsey_key_to_lsu_defense, Oct. 6,
2009.

73   By age 8, though, . . . for him to play.: McCartney, "A Tiger Unchained,"
p. 48.

73   "despicable, vile, unprincipled scoundrels.": MacArthur, p. 152.

73   To know where he's come . . . like a miracle to me.: McCartney, "A Tiger
Unchained," p. 47.

74   The population of Walnut Grove . . . at least learn to dribble.": "For Gunter,
40th Season as Good as the First," *LSU Campus: LSU Highlights Spring 2004*,
http://www.lsu.edu/highlights/041/gunter.html, Feb. 4, 2010.

74   before nearly 15,000 fans, . . . it came true that day.": Randy Rosetta,
"Gunter Was an Inspiration to Friends, Colleagues," *The Advocate*, Aug. 5,
2005, http://docs.newsbank.com/s/InfoWeb/aggdocs/NewsBank.

75   "Husbands and wives . . . anything better to do.": Carl Dubois, "Tigers
Hoping for One More Lap at The Box," *The Advocate*, May 12, 2008, http://
docs.newsbank.com/s/InfoWeb/aggdocs/NewsBank, Jan. 21, 2010.

75   Athletic Director Skip Bertman peeled . . . slapping hands with the fans.:
Dubois, "Tigers Hoping."

75   Bertman asked the fans . . . Still to Come!": Dubois, "Tigers Hoping."

75   It was a tremendous facility in its day.: Sam King, "A Box Full of Memories," *The Advocate*, May 4, 2008, http://docs.newsbank.com/s/InfoWeb/
aggdocs/NewsBank, Jan. 21, 2010.

76   "All we hoped to do . . . was keep football alive,": Hardesty, p. 145.

76   Moore told reporters he . . . the season, was healthy.: Hardesty, p. 145.

76   No rail accommodations . . . his lot and sold them.: Hardesty, pp. 147-48.

76   I don't remember what . . . to travel in style.: Hardesty, p. 148.

77   "I wasn't even thinking I might be going in,": Mule, *Game of My Life*,
p. 50.

77   "The seemingly almost-forgotten backup . . . turning on a light switch,":
Mule, *Game of My Life*, p. 51.

77   "What we needed . . . was our emotional leader.": Mule, *Game of My Life*,
p. 53.

77   Saban said he had never . . . to a backup player.: Mule, *Game of My Life*,
p. 56.

77   Surprise might not be . . . more than just surprised.: Mule, *Game of My Life*,
p. 50.

78   Softball coach Yvette Girouard made . . . of a standing ovation.: William
Weathers, "Curtain Call," *The Advocate*, June 1, 2004, http://docs.newsbank.

com/s/InfoWeb/aggdocs/NewsBank, Jan. 20, 2010.

78   Schmidt intended to pitch . . . for the final game.: Weathers, "Curtain Call."

78   "I saw her do it . . . everything that's in me.": Weathers, "Curtain Call."

78   Kudos to our sport . . . certainly deserved that.: Weathers, "Curtain Call."

79   Moore had a sharp mind . . . ever saw him swallow it.: Hardesty, p. 112.

80   had managed to "sneak" . . . some favorable tiebreakers.: Feinswog, p. 14.

80   Tiger cornerback Randall Gay . . . to break up the pass.: Feinswog, p. 15.

81   "six-year soaking in the depths of an ocean of defeat.": Sam King, "This Too Good to Be Dream," *The Advocate*, March 20, 2000, http://docs.news bank.com/s/InfoWeb/aggdocs/NewsBank, Jan 19, 2010.

81   "couldn't be a dream" . . . aren't this good.": King, "This Too Good."

81   He chose to play . . . necessary to win.: King, "This Too Good."

81   If I would have . . . laughed me out of town.: King, "This Too Good."

82   With half a dozen reserves in the lineup: Bud Montet, "Tigers Rally to Lasso Wyoming, 20-13," *The Greatest Moments in LSU Football History*, Francis J. Fitzgerald, ed. (Champaign, IL: Sports Publishing L.L.C., 2002), p. 61.

82   It's not where you're picked but where you finish.: Warner, p. 159.

83   "a marquee matchup . . . nation's stingiest defenses.": *Tiger Terrific!*, p. 58.

83   "The quarterback is the starter . . . it makes a difference." *Tiger Terrific!*, p. 60.

84   During the fall of 2002, . . . never interfered with his pitching.: Carl Dubois, "Learning to Slow Down," *The Advocate*, June 1, 2005, http://docs. newsbank.com/s/InfoWeb/aggdocs/NewsBank, Jan. 20, 2010.

84   It scared the heck out of us.: Dubois, "Learning to Slow Down."

85   the LSU Tigers became the . . . a game on foreign soil: Mule, *Eye of the Tiger*, p. 26.

85   The Cubans apparently wanted . . . fruit of the vine.: Mule, *Eye of the Tiger*, p. 27.

85   LSU's great George "Doc" . . . swim out of there.": Mule, *Eye of the Tiger*, p. 28.

86   Not a drop of rain . . . Charlie "Choo Choo" Justice.: Hardesty, p. 162.

86   A groundskeeper always watered . . . and stopped him.: Hardesty, p. 162.

86   Both teams played on . . . was LSU's Zollie Toth.: Hardesty, p. 162.

87   his father, Press, announced . . . what they called "Showtime.": Mark Kriegel, "The Pistol," *Sports Illustrated*, Jan. 8, 2007, http://sportsillustrated. cnn.com/vault/article/magazine/MAG1116086, Nov. 1, 2009.

88   Lord, what do we do now? . . . that drew chaos near.: Marvin West, "In a Difficult Hour, the Torch Is Passed," *The Greatest Moments in LSU Football History*, Francis J. Fitzgerald, ed (Champaign, IL: Sports Publishing L.L.C., 2002), p. 108.

88   Dietzel spent more than a year searching for a successor. West, p. 107.

88   Rein brought energy . . . from a recruiting trip.: West, p. 107.

88   The plane veered off course, . . . LSU to the foundations,": West, p. 108.

88   With recruiting at its peak, . . . and pay three staffs.: West, p. 108.

88   I would gladly surrender . . . could still be here.: West, p. 110.

89   "I hadn't solidified . . . fortify my starting role.": Feinswog, p. 4.

89   A local dentist led . . . my mind was right.": Feinswog, p. 5.

89   "The only thing I have . . . grew over the years,: Feinswog,

p. 5.

89   People just thought . . . my tongue and played.: Feinswog, p. 5.

90   "The game was without . . . their defeat good-humoredly.": Hardesty, p. 20.

90   "quickly turned into . . . but blood-broiling.": Mule, *Eye of the Tiger*, p. 9.

90   "Tulane's third team was better than our first team.": Mule, *Eye of the Tiger*, p. 18.

90   Things change. So no hard feelings.: Tammy Nunez, "Tulane Athletic Director Rick Dickson Reacts," *The Times-Picayune*, Sept. 16, 2009, http://www.nola.com/tulane/index.ssf/2009/09/tulane_athletic_director_rick.html, Sept. 23, 2009.

BIBLIOGRAPHY

"1976-77: The Only Lady Tigers to Reach the National Championship Game of a Post-Season Tournament." *2006-07 LSU Women's Basketball Media Guide*. 147. http://www.lsusports.net/ViewArticle.dbml.

Anderson, Kelli. "Beware of Tigers." *Sports Illustrated*. 24 March 2008. http://sportsillustrated.cnn.com/vault/article/magazine/MAG1127561/index.htm.

---. "Home Is Where the Heart Is." *Sports Illustrated*. 19 Sept. 2005. http://vault.sportsillustrated.cnn.com/vault/article/magazine/MAG1106374/index.htm.

Ballard, Bernell. "Tigers Stun Ole Miss, Orange Bowl Brass." *Greatest Moments in LSU Football History*. Francis J. Fitzgerald, ed. Champaign, IL: Sports Publishing L.L.C., 2002. 89.

Bettinger, Jim & Julie S. *The Book of Bowden*. Nashville: TowleHouse Publishing, 2001.

"Bob Pettit." *Wikipedia, the free encyclopedia*. http://en.wikipedia.org/wiki/Bob_Pettit.

Calongne, Kristine. "After 15 Years, LSU-Auburn Game Still an Earthshaking Experience." *LSU Campus: LSU Highlights Winter2003*. http://www.lsu.edu/highlights/033/football.html.

Davis, John K. "Glenn Dorsey: Key to LSU Defense." *suite101.com*. 5 Jan. 2008. http://college-football.suite101.com/article/cfm/glenn_dorsey_key_to_lsu_defense.

Deville, Matt. "Girouard, LSU Ready to Take the Field at New Tiger Park." *TigerRag.com*. 11 Feb. 2009. http://www.tigerrag.com/?p=6661.

"Dominance on the Track." *2010 LSU Track & Field Media Guide*. LSUsports.net. 10.

Dubois, Carl. "Game Too Early for Some." *The Advocate*. 31 Aug. 2008. http://docs.newsbank.com/s/InfoWeb/aggdocs/NewsBank.

---. "Learning to Slow Down: LSU Left-Hander Smith Overcoming Condition That Causes Rapid Heartbeat." *The Advocate*. 1 June 2005. http://docs.newsbank.com/s/InfoWeb/aggdocs/NewsBank.

---. "LSU Opener Anything But Normal." *The Advocate*. 31 Aug. 2008. http://docs.newsbank.com/s/InfoWeb/aggdocs/NewsBank.

---. "Tigers Hoping for One More Lap at The Box." *The Advocate*. 12 May 2008. http://docs.newsbank.com/s/InfoWeb/aggdocs/NewsBank.

Feinswog, Lee. *Tales from the LSU Sidelines: A Captivating Collection of Tiger Football Stories*. Champaign, IL: Sports Publishing L.L.C., 2002.

"For Gunter, 40th Season as Good as the First." *LSU Campus: LSU Highlights Spring 2004*. http://www.lsu.edu/highlights/041/gunter.html.

Guilbeau, Glenn. "Amazing: Dream Comes True as LSU Wins Thriller for Fifth

194

National Title." *The Advocate*. 18 June 2000. http://docs.newsbank.com/s/InfoWeb/aggdocs/NewsBank.

---. "Top 10 Games of Bertman Era." *The Advocate*. 13 May 2001. http://docs.newsbank.com/s/InfoWeb/aggdocs/NewsBank.

Hardesty, Dan. *The Louisiana Tigers: LSU Football*. Huntsville, AL: The Strode Publishers, 1975.

Helman, David. "Softball: Current, Former Tigers Excited About Stadium Advancements." *Daily Reveille*. 16 Feb. 2009. http://www.lsureveille.com/softball-current-former-tigers-excited-about-stadium-advancements.

Hendrickson, Brian. "LSU Fans Prove to Be a Class Act in Regionals." *Wilmington Star-News*. 2 June 2003. reprinted in *The Advocate*. 22 June 2003. http://docs.newsbank.com/s/InfoWeb/aggdocs/NewsBank.

Hunter, Bruce. *Don't Count Me Out: The Irrepressible Dale Brown and His LSU Fighting Tigers*. Chicago: Bonus Books, Inc. 1989.

Hunter, Bruce and Joe Planas. *Fighting Tigers Basketball: Great LSU Teams, Players and Traditions*. Chicago: Bonus Books, Inc., 1991.

Hyams, Jimmy. "Risher & Tigers Upset Alabama, 20-10." *Greatest Moments in LSU Football History*. Francis J. Fitzgerald, ed. Champaign, IL: Sports Publishing L.L.C., 2002. 112-15.

King. Sam. "Bertman Believes This One May Be Best Yet." *The Advocate*. 18 June 2000. http://docs.newsbank.com/s/InfoWeb/aggdocs/NewsBank.

---. "A Box Full of Memories." *The Advocate*. 4 May 2008. http://docs.newsbank.com/s/InfoWeb/aggdocs/Newsbank.

---. "This Too Good to Be Dream." *The Advocate*. 20 March 2000. http://docs.newsbank.com/s/InfoWeb/aggdocs/NewsBank.

Kirkpatrick, Curry. "Shack Attack." *Sports Illustrated*. 21 Jan. 1991. http://sportsillustrated.cnn.com/vault/article/magazine/MAG1118770/index.htm.

"Know Your Softball Tigers -- Anissa Young and Kirsten Shortridge." *LSUsports.net*. 2 Feb. 2009. http://www.lsusports.net/ViewArticle.dbml.

Kriegel, Mark. "The Pistol." *Sports Illustrated*. 8 Jan. 2007. http://sportsillustrated.cnn.com/vault/article/magazine/MAG1116086.

Lawrence, Andrew. "Golden Oldie." *Sports Illustrated Presents LSU Tigers: 2007 National Champions*. 16 Jan. 2008. 55-57.

Lowe, Kent, Sr. "Look Back: 20 Years after LSU, Loyola Marymount." *LSUsports.net*. 3 Feb. 2010. http://www.lsusports.net/ViewArticle.dbml.

"LSU Football Traditions A to Z." *2009 LSU Football Media Guide*. 60-65.http://www.lsusports.net/ViewArticle.dbml.

MacArthur, John. *Twelve Ordinary Men*. Nashville: W Publishing Group, 2002.

MacMahon, Tim. "Brandon Bass' Camp Is Just the Beginning." *Dallas Mavericks Blog*. 21 June 2008. http://mavsblog.dallasnews.com/archives/2008/06.

McCartney, Cory. "One Title Down, One More to Go." *Sports Illustrated Presents LSU Tigers: 2007 National Champions*. 16 Jan. 2008. 35.

---. "A Tiger Unchained." *Sports Illustrated Presents LSU Tigers: 2007 National Champions*. 16 Jan. 2008. 47-49.

Mickles, Sheldon. "Right on Track: Lady Tigers Capture 25th Track Trophy." *The Advocate*. 15 June 2008. http://docs.newsbank.com/s/InfoWeb/aggdocs/NewsBank.

Montet, Bud. "Tigers Rally to Lasso Wyoming 20-13." *The Greatest Moments in LSU Football History*. Francis J. Fitzgerald, ed. Champaign, IL: Sports Publishing L.L.C., 2002. 60-61.

Mule, Marty. *Eye of the Tiger: A Hundred Years of LSU Football.* Atlanta: Longstreet Press, 1993.

---. *Game of My Life: LSU: Memorable Stories of Tigers Football.* Champaign, IL: Sports Publishing L.L.C., 2006.

Murphy, Austin. "The 2007 BCS Championship." *Sports Illustrated Presents LSU Tigers: 2007 National Champions.* 16 Jan. 2008. 36-44.

Nunez, Tammy. "Tulane Athletic Director Rick Dickson Reacts to the End of the Tulane-LSU Football Series." *The Times-Picayune.* 16 Sept. 2009. http://www.nola.com/tulane/index.ssf/2009/09/tulane_athletic_director_rick.html.

Rabalais, Scott. "LSU Comeback Beyond Words." *The Advocate.* 31 March 2003. http://docs.newsbank.com/s/InfoWeb/aggdocs/NewsBank.

---. "LSU Stays Alive with High Drama." *The Advocate.* 21 May 2000. http://docs.newsbank.com/s/InfoWeb/aggdocs/NewsBank.

---. "LSU's Robinson Enjoys Practice: Relishes Chance to Play Game He Almost Lost." *The Advocate.* 26 March 2002. http://docs.newsbank.com/s/InfoWeb/aggdocs/NewsBank.

Rosetta, Randy. "Big Makeover: A Slimmer and Trimmer Davis Motivated to Give Tigers Boost." *The Advocate.* 30 July 2006. http://docs.newsbank.com/s/InfoWeb/aggdocs/NewsBank.

---. "Giving Back: Bass Helping Underprivileged at Camp." *The Advocate.* 18 July 2008. http://docs.newsbank.com/s/InfoWeb/aggdocs/NewsBank.

---. "Gunter Was an Inspiration to Friends, Colleagues." *The Advocate.* 5 Aug. 2005. http://docs.newsbank/com/s/InfoWeb/aggdocs/NewsBank.

---. "Happy to Be There: LSU's Barksdale Doesn't Regret Moving from Defensive to Offensive Line." *The Advocate.* 10 Sept. 2008. http://docs.newsbank.com/s/InfoWeb/aggdocs/Newsbank.

---. "Miles Never Considered Conceding TD to State." *The Advocate.* 28 Sept. 2009. http://docs.newsbank.com/s/InfoWeb/aggdocs/NewsBank.

---. "Ochinko Delivers After Move to Clean-Up." *The Advocate.* 25 June 2009. http://www.2theadvocate.com/sports/lsu/49056876.html.

---. "Playing with Pain: Pittman Misses Late Brother." *The Advocate.* 20 Aug. 2006. http://docs.newsbank.com/s/InfoWeb/aggdocs/NewsBank.

---. "Source of Strength: LSU Offensive Lineman, Young, Ailing Boy Inspire Each Other." *The Advocate.* 25 Dec. 2009. http://docs.newsbank.com/s/InfoWeb/aggdocs/NewsBank.

---. "Taking a Stand: Goal-Line Stop Lifts LSU Past MSU." *The Advocate.* 27 Sept. 2009. http://docs.newsbank.com/s/InfoWeb/aggdocs/NewsBank.

---. "Tigers Ecstatic about Chance to Play for Title." *The Advocate.* 3 Dec. 2007. http://docs.newsbank.com/s/InfoWeb/aggdocs/Newsbank.

"Saturday Night in Death Valley." *2009 LSU Football Media Guide.* 34-35. http://www.lsusports.net/ViewArticle.dmbl.

"Shoot out the Moon: More to Pete Maravich Than the 'Pistol.'" *LSU Campus: LSU Highlights Spring 2005.* http://www.lsu.edu/highlights/051/maravich.html.

"Tiger Stadium." *2009 LSU Football Media Guide.* 184-87. http://www.lsusports.net/ViewArticle.dmbl.

Tiger Terrific! LSU's Unforgettable 2003 Championship Season. Chicago: Triumph Books, 2004.

Warner, Chris, ed. *SEC Sports Quotes.* Baton Rouge: CEW Enterprises, 2002.

"Warren Morris." *TheGoal.com.* http://www.thegoal.com/players/baseball/morris_

196

warren/morris21_warren.html.

Weathers, William. "Curtain Call: MVP Schmidt Savoring Cheers of Marathon Day." *The Advocate*. 1 June 2004. http://docs.newsbank.com/s/InfoWeb/aggdocs/ NewsBank.

West, Marvin. "In a Difficult Hour, the Torch Is Passed." *The Greatest Moments in LSU Football History*. Francis J. Fitzgerald, ed. Champaign, IL: Sports Publishing L.L.C., 2002. 106-111.

Wickes, Frank B. "LSU Band History." *LSU Department of Bands*. http://www.bands. lsu.edu/band_history/index.php.

INDEX
(LAST NAME, DEVOTION DAY NUMBER)

Aaron, Hank 18
Abrahamson, Michael 22
Addai, Joseph 7
Alexander, Charles 19
Arnsparger, Bill 89
Ashe, Arthur 37
Augustus, Seimone 26
Baker, Ryan 64
Banks, Tommy 14, 77
Bannister, Sir Roger 80
Baptiste, Kelly 16
Barbier, Blair 60
Barksdale, Joseph 58
Barrow, Wylie M. 31
Barton, Kirk 73
Bartram, Dave 51
Bass, Bill 48
Bass, Brandon 37
Beckwith, Darry 22
Bernstein, Joe 35
Bertman, Sandy 75
Bertman, Skip 24, 60, 74, 75
Betanzos, Juan Carlos 70
Bible, Dana X. 55
Bird, Leo 51
Black, Ciron 32
Blair, Nathan 49
Blanton, Ricky 12, 56
Booty, Josh 77
Bowden, Bobby 15, 23, 45, 49, 64
Bowman, Scotty 5
Boyd, Annie 45
Boyd, Brad 11
Brady, John 81, 82
Bridges, Rocky 74
Brown, Dale 12, 21, 56, 63, 71
Brown, Vonnie 56
Bryant, Bear 6, 51, 70

Burns, Craig 38
Cannon, Billy 17, 24, 30, 73
Carazo, Castro 31
Casanova, Tommy 8, 38
Chambers, Mike 69
Chancellor, Van 6
Clark, Ryan 77
Clayton, Michael 3, 7, 83
Coates, Charles E. 1
Cohen, Russ 23
Cook, Beano 72
Corbett, Jim 44, 48, 61
Crass, Bill 15
Cresse, Brad 60
Cusimano, Charles 90
Daniels, Travis 80
Dantin, Chris 11
Dark, Alvin 36
Davey, Rohan 77, 80
Davis, Brad 11
Davis, Domanick 80
Davis, Glen 33
Davis, Wendell 5, 54
de Lench, Brooke 26
Dean, Blake 2
Dean, Joe 60
Dentmon, Justin 66
Dickson, Rick 90
Dietzel, Paul 8, 17, 30, 44, 46, 59, 88
DiNardo, Gerry 14
Donaldson, Cedrick 14
Dorsey, Glenn 13, 73
Dorsey, Sandra 73
Doucet, Early 66
Doughtery, Nora 45
Douglass, Dee 52
Dutton, Tom 35
Eddy, Shawn 84
Ellen, Don 48

Eumont, Vic 19
Fatherree, Jesse 15
Faulk, Kevin 14
Feldman, Bruce 50
Fenton, George 85
Fiser, Jack 69
Fisher, J.S. 31
Fisher, Jimbo 3, 77
Fitzgerald, Sara 78
Flynn, Matt 4, 13
Foley, Art 23
Fontenot, Mike 60
Fowles, Sylvia 6
Fuller, Eddie 50
Furniss, Eddy 24
Gauthreaux, Essie 45
Gay, Randall 80
Gillespie, Gordie 24
Girouard, Yvette 10, 78
Goode, Burt 76
Gottlieb, Lewis 76
Green, Jarvis 20
Green, Skyler 66
Griffin, Benny 82
Gunter, Sue 26, 74
Harris, Wendell 30
Hastings, Stephanie 52
Heard, Red 23, 65
Heard, T.P. 41, 72
Henderson, Devery 3, 7, 83
Henry, Samantha 16
Hester, Jacob 57
Higginbotham, Wm. 43
Hilliard, Dalton 53, 70
Hodges, Doneeka 26
Hodson, Tommy 27, 50, 54, 89
Holt, Glenn 5

Howell, Ida 45
Hunter, Dr. John 44
Jackson, Chris 63
Jackson, Chris 83
Jackson, Gus 35
Jackson, Maree 18
Jackson, Rusty 11
Jefferson, Jordan 64
Johnson, Brian 66
Jones, Bert 11
Jones, Biff 9, 65
Jones, Chad 64
Joseph, Jerry 48
Justice, Charlie 86
Karsten, Adrian 40
Kavanaugh, Ken 51
Keigley, Gerald 11
Kinchen, Brian 27
Kinchen, Gary 27
Kinchen, Gaynell 27
Kinchen, Todd 27
Kinchen, Toni 27
King, Sam 81
Kizer, Roland 35
Konz, Ken 41
Labruzzo, Joe 48
LaFell, Brandon 4, 22
Landry, Jo Ann 53
Laval, Smoke 84
Lawrence, Deonna 16
LeBlanc, RaShonda 6
LeDoux, Jimmy 11
Lemmon, Jack 21
Lewis, Ashley 52
Lewis, Terry 54
Lindsey, Lloyd 49
Lombardi, Vince 16, 46
Long, Huey 9, 23, 25,
   31, 65
Lyles, W.M. 85
Maine, Winnie 45
Mainieri, Paul 2
Manning, Archie 38
Manning, Eli 83
Maravich, Pete 29, 49, 87
Maravich, Press 56, 87
Mauck, Matt 7, 80, 83
McArdle, Benny 71
McClendon, Charles 8,
   11, 17, 19, 38, 44, 48, 70,
   71, 79, 82, 88
McCormick, Dave 48
McDonnell, E.T. 55
McFarland, Reggie 35

McGraw, Leon 75
McGraw, Tug 31
McKowen, Lucille 45
Mickal, Abe 9, 15, 65
Mike the Tiger 43, 69
Miles, Les 22, 28, 57,
   58, 64
Milner, Riley 50
Mitchell, Jared 2
Moody, Darrell 53
Moore, Bernie 51, 76, 79
Moore, Glenn 52
Moreau, Doug 36, 48
Morel, Tommy 82
Morgan, H.A. 1
Morris, Brooklynn 16
Morris, Warren 67
Mule, Marty 27
Murrill, Paul 88
Newton, Stacey 52
Nitschke, Ray 79
Nix, Buddy 53
Noll, Chuck 12
Norwood, Lula 45
Ochinko, Sean 2
Ohanaja, Jessica 16
O'Neal, Shaquille 21, 33,
   37, 63
Paige, Leroy 7
Perrilloux, Ryan 28
Pettit, Bob 39
Phillips, W.J. 45
Phillips, W. Keith Jr. 38
Pittman, Chase 68
Pittman, Cole 68
Pleasant, Ruffin G. 31
Pontiff, Wally 60
Pray, Irving 55
Rabb, Warren 30
Rabenhorst, Harry 71
Randall, Marcus 3
Reed, Josh 77
Reeves, Jennie 52
Reid, Mike 47
Rein, Bo 88
Reynolds, Jerry 12
Richards, Bob 85
Rios, Armando 24
Risher, Alan 70
Roberts, Stanley 63
Robinson, Reggie 34
Roessner, Killian 10
Rogers, Will 65
Roshto, Jim 86

Russell, JaMarcus 4, 66
Ruth, Babe 18, 83
Saban, Nick 34, 62, 77, 80
Schembechler, Bo 28
Schmidt, Kristin 78
Schuelke, Jennifer 52
Scott, Edwin A. 25
Scott, Malcolm 70
Shaver, Dennis 16
Sheppard, Kelvin 64
Shilton, Peter 35
Shortridge, Kirsten 10
Simmons, Albert P. 1
Smith, Aiysha 26
Smith, Glenn 82
Smith, Greg 84
Smith, Jabari 81
Spears, Marcus 83
Stargell, Willie 34
Steltz, Craig 13
Stokley, Nelson 8, 82
Stovall, Jerry 46, 53, 70, 88
Studrawa, Greg 58
Swift, Stromile 81
Taylor, Jim 57
Theriot, Ryan 60
Thomas, LaTavia 16
Tinsley, Gaynell 15, 27,
   41, 65, 86
Tittle, Y.A. 61
Toefield, LaBrandon 80
Toth, Zollie 86
Toups, Al 63
Turner, Emily 10
Tyler, Herb 14
Van Buren, Steve 76
Vincent, Herb 27
Vincent, Justin 62
Wade, Malcolm 49
Walker, Todd 24
Ward, Steve 59
White, DeTrina 26
White, Jason 62
Wilkinson, Bud 9, 41
Williams, John 12
Wilson, Nickiesha 16
Wilson, Nikita 12
Wingard, Edgar 45, 85
Witten, Jeremy 60
Wooden, John 87
Woods, Al 64
Zatopek, Emil 67
Zenon, Jonathan 28
Zeringue, Jon 42